Time
TO REFLECT

LAURA FALK

Produced by:

FriesenPress

Suite 300 – 852 Fort Street
Victoria, BC, Canada V8W 1H8

www.friesenpress.com

Distributed to the trade by The Ingram Book Company

Table of Contents

Introduction and Appreciation

This small book has been written with you in mind. I have included a title called "Lingering in the Lines" to encourage you to participate with God in developing your spiritual life. It is a privilege to have you reading these small writings that I have written over a period of ten years. I wrote these articles for our bookstore and had them printed in our local newspaper. Thank you to all you who have encouraged me to put these writings into a book. I have listened to your challenge and here it is. There will be repetitions in the thoughts communicated but may each repetition be another reminder to love God and His truth.

I wish to express a note of gratitude to all the people that have come to the café Bible studies and women conferences that our bookstore hosts. I have appreciated you all and it truly is an honour to know you. To a lovely group of women who are "gripped" by God. We share a sweet "fellowship" with each other. We have shared our sorrows, our joys, our questions, and our encouragement. We have entered God and His truth into every issue and I deeply respect that in each one of you. You are cherished and I want you to know that.

I also desire to express my profound appreciation for a host of friends who come alongside and help with the women conferences that we plan. You are valued, loved, and needed. Thank you for your prayers and selfless involvement to do the work required. I am trusting that you who have been on a conference planning team will receive this heartfelt sentiment. I know that eternity will show all of your individual efforts rewarded by God Himself. Thank you to our staff for faithfully working with us.

Dedications

I dedicate this book to the memory of my beloved parents HENRY and HANNAH NEUFELD whose love for God shaped my own. My parents were known simply as people who loved. There truly is no greater legacy to be had. My siblings and our children shared these wonderful people. The legacy lives on! Oh, to see their faces once again!

To my husband, Dale, without whose help, the manuscript would never have been sent off to the printer. Your faithful love has been a deep blessing in my life and for your support in all God calls me to do, I thank you.

To my children and their spouses (Dave & Kristie, Janel & Donovan, and Kevin) who truly are gifts from God. I am so grateful to have shared this earth with your presence. Thank you for creating the flower garden and for the gift of the chair. I spend many hours sitting there with thoughts of you and prayers for you. Your deep regard and respect for me is a gift I do not deserve but deeply appreciate. Thank you to my daughter for her professional expertise in this book project.

Thank you to the women who have asked me to mentor you and to those that invited me to tell my story. I don't think you realize how much that asking has grown my walk with God. Thank you for being real and sharing your stories with me. I consider it a privilege to share life with you even in some small part. It is God's truth applied that changes us and you have allowed that to happen. The applause of heaven is heard as you walk humbly with your God.

In Honour To

I write this book in honour of and glory to the King eternal, immortal, invisible, the only God, forever and ever.

He called me by name, touching my heart and changing my life with His words, "I have loved you with an everlasting love." That is enough! Thank you Lord!

In Contrast

There are two ways we can be according to God's Word. We can be flourishing or diminishing. We can be constantly longing or deeply satisfied. In Jeremiah Chapter 17 it says that when we trust in our own strength and turn away from God we are like a bush in a wasteland and do not see prosperity when it comes. We develop the bad attitude of negativity. This attitude causes us to grumble about everything and appreciate nothing. Our relationships start to suffer because our negative attitudes make it hard for people to be around us. God likens this way of living to being like a bush in the salt land of a parched desert. Here in this place the bush is not flourishing. The salt place causes thirst but there is no water to quench that thirst.

God goes on to contrast this truth with another story of how *"Blessed is the man whose trust and confidence is in the Lord. He will be like a tree planted by the water with strong roots and green leaves and always fruit bearing."* Here in this place of faith and confidence in God the thirst of doubt and worry is quenched. Here in this place of faith and confidence in God the thirst for value, purpose and meaning is quenched. There is never a shortage of water when the One who calls Himself the Living Water is watering your life.

LINGERING in the LINES – Read Isaiah 58

Intimacy with Regard

God is your very best Friend. Jesus was speaking about Himself in John 14 when He said, "*Greater love has no one than this, that He lay down His life for His friends. You are my friends if you do what I command.*" Stop a moment and reread the above quote from the very mouth of God.

Jesus calls you His friend. Jesus put aside all of His own comfort and laid down His life for you His friend. By laying down His life Jesus took the blame for every wrong you will ever do or have done. Jesus did that. Jesus took His perfect character of God and became sin for you even though He was never guilty of any wrong doing. Now, that is a friend indeed. Jesus told us that we were His friends if we would do what He commands. On the surface that may seem like a string attached to God's declaration of loving friendship but it's not.

This is Jesus telling us to receive His sacrifice into our lives so that we can have a friendship with God. Friendship is always a two-way street of sharing our lives with one another in connection, community, and conversation. This is the definition of friendship.

Jesus, the holy God called Saviour, laid down His life for us and we need to bow our knee to Him with deep regard. Jesus, the holy man called Friend, warmly embraces you with His unfailing love and acceptance. His embrace weeps with you when you weep and rejoices over you. Now, that is a Friend to desire, to receive, and sing over.

LINGERING in the LINES – Read Romans 5

A Confidence Kept

In Hebrews 10:35 we are told not to throw away our confidence in God's truth because in keeping this confidence we will be richly rewarded. God's character of truth makes His words of truth something I can count on. When God says we are forgiven we are forgiven (I John 1:9). This is a confidence keeping truth. When God says we have a future in heaven prepared for us then we have a future in heaven awaiting us (John 14:2).

When God says I can do all things through Christ who gives me strength then I can do what God wants me to do (Philippians 4:13). I can love and I can forgive and I can be generous. When God says that He will do more than I could ask or imagine then He will (Ephesians 3:20). When God says that He is doing a new thing then He is doing a new thing and our job is to see it (Isaiah 43:19). This is your confidence kept declaration and resolution. So don't throw it away. Because if you do you'll miss the reward of seeing these promises fulfilled in your life. Let us purpose to be Confidence Keepers!

LINGERING in the LINES – Read Acts 2

All in the Family

God is good. God is merciful. God is kind. God is compassionate. God is love. God is embracing. God is faithful. God is committed. God is generous. God is for you. God is good. God never takes advantage of people. Yet, in the story of the prodigal son the older son feels that his father is taking advantage of him. He feels unloved and unappreciated. He feels that somehow his father has withheld good things from him. And yet none of His thoughts are true of our God in heaven. Jesus told this story in the Bible so we could see that our attitudes about God are wrong when not based on the truth of His Word.

According to the story suddenly there was a division in the family when the younger son runs off to a far off place. In that place the son squanders the wealth of an inheritance he was given. The older son stayed at home to work on the farm with his father. He was present with his father in proximity and yet due to the wrong views about his father he was as far away from his father's heart as the younger son was from his father's home.

Are you present with God yet far away from home because you are doing things for God with a heart of duty and drudgery? Have wrong views of God based on fickle feelings taken you away from the real home of God's heart? If this is true of you then just do what the younger son in the story did and come home. Come home to the Father. Come home in heart! God is good, always good (Luke 15).

LINGERING in the LINES – Read Isaiah 1

Build a Prayer

Genesis 1 is the story of how God created the world and everything in it. The Creator longs to create alongside us and this story teaches us how to pray. In the beginning the earth was formless, empty and dark. That is exactly what our lives are when we do not pray. Prayer is created as we speak words to our God. "Lord, I am confused over this dark situation in my life and ask for You to speak Your words 'Let there be light' over my darkness. I need to see and only Your light will help me to do so. Enlighten me with the counsel of Your Word. Amen."

The prayer creation continues as we speak "Lord, You separated the water from water and called the expanse sky and the dry ground land. This tells me God that You are above us in all things and that Your view is higher than our earthly thoughts. So bring Your heavenly answers to the land of my need. Amen." God's created work took time to grow and flourish and so does prayer.

"Lord, You created the land to produce fruit with seeds to keep my character growing into the design of Your image of love, holiness, patience, kindness, humility, strength, peace, and power. May I plant continual seeds of Your truth into my life by applying Your truth to my situations. May I leave a legacy of You here on earth as I spread Your seeds on every road of earth I step. Amen." So, my challenge to you is to "Build a Prayer" in your life by taking the active, living, and powerful Word of God and moving those words into active, living, and powerful prayer.

LINGERING in the LINES – Write out a prayer according to Romans 12

Do I Know You?
Based on Luke 13

Jesus tells the people around Him a little story about what salvation in Christ is all about. Jesus tells the people to make every effort to enter through the narrow door because many will try to enter and will not be able to. The people do not understand what Jesus is saying here because they think they are good with God. These people tell Jesus that they ate and drank with Jesus hearing Jesus teach in their streets. But despite their words Jesus will tell these people that He does not know them.

To know Jesus as our Lord and Saviour we cannot eat WITH Him in just hearing His truth spoken to us. We must eat OF Christ by applying God's truth to our lives. This is how we will know God and how He will know us. This mutual knowing is we seeking God and God finding us. This mutual knowing is we asking of God and God asking of us. This mutual knowing is we knocking on the door of His heart and God knocking on the door of our heart.

Don't let an illusion of knowing God be your story. Don't think walking into a church building is enough. Don't think that reading a comforting story from the Bible is enough. Don't ignore the Bible verses that speak of your personal sin and the need to make things right with you and God. Don't ignore Jesus.

If you don't ignore God you will find life for your soul and truth for your confusions. I know this because Jesus calls Himself the Way, the Truth, and the Life (John 14:6).

LINGERING in the LINES – Read Matthew 7

Do You See
What I See?

God wants us to be confident in His loving care. He wants us to be confident of our citizenship in heaven as His redeemed beloved children. God wants us to be confident to face our fears and weakness with His strength and courage moving us forward. God wants us to be confident to know and use the gifts and abilities He has given us. God applauds us when our confidence is in Him and in who He is and in what He can do.

What God does not applaud but abhors is pride that we somehow choose to disguise as confidence. Pride is mentioning all your gifts and abilities instead of quietly using them for God's purpose. The Bible tells us to let praises for our efforts to come from lips that are not our own (Proverbs 27:2). Pride is thinking that your gifts are exclusive and no one could possibly have similar abilities. Pride is always exalting self and self efforts.

Confidence is realizing that we are unworthy to receive anything from God. Confidence tells us that despite our weakness and frailties God is good and loves us and wants to give good gifts to His children. Confidence is God always having first place in everything we are and do. Confidence is the humility to realize that it is God and God alone who gives us our abilities. Confidence is the humility to realize it is God alone who causes our abilities given to us to be activated for His designed purposes (Deuteronomy 8:17, 18). With this kind of confidence you are free to be and free to do!

LINGERING in the LINES – Read Romans 8

Everyone Works

I was scheduled to run my first ten kilometre relay run for a charity and had never accepted a challenge like this before. I had done the work of training and yet the struggle of running was a stress and a worry. Then I got a word from a friend. She pulled me aside and told me she was going to pray for me every 15 minutes while I was running this race. That declaration from a friend to pray to the God of heaven and earth stirred my heart in courage and resolve. I would do the work of the run with its various turns and curves along the way. She would do the work of prayer. God would do the work of sending down the answer.

In a sense, prayer is a ten kilometre run of its own. It is a race we agree to do. I agreed to race and my friend agreed to pray. We were committed to a cause. Praying takes time and it is intentional work. The race takes time until you have run the distance needed to cross the finish line. There is no race unless you run. There is no prayer unless you pray. There are new curves and turns in the road called prayer. You may desire to pray a certain way and God redirects it to a new curve. The Bible says to pray in the Spirit on all occasions. The Spirit of God knows what we should pray and we only think we know. The redirection is necessary for the prayer to be effective (Ephesians 6:18).

There is sweat in running and in prayer. It is ceaseless in its work until the issue is settled with the finish line of an answer. The Bible says that whatever you do, you are to work at it with all of your heart as working for the Lord and not for men (Colossians 3:23).

LINGERING in the LINES – Read I Kings 8

Highway to Heaven

God is never surprised at anything that comes your way. God is alive, awake and aware. This is your comfort in the issues of life. The following verses from the Bible show this comfort that God can bring to us.

Job 23:10—But He knows the way I take.

Psalm 25:12—God instructs His beloved in the way chosen for them.

Psalm 138:8—The Lord will fulfill His purpose for me.

Hebrews 12:1—Let us run the race marked out for us.

God knows. God knows what is happening. He has worked ahead of time to help you run the race that is marked out for you. God will fulfill His purpose for your life. He knows the purpose He has for you. God knows the way you take. God knows the way to fulfill His purpose for you. God knows. God knows and promises to instruct you on how to do your life journey (Psalm 32:8). When you make mistakes God knows. God will forgive and reweave things to get you back on His purposeful plan for you. God has you covered in every way (Psalm 139). Be comforted in the truth that God knows.

LINGERING in the LINES – Read Psalm 138

I Have a Friend

Sometimes our attitude is wrong and we know it. When that happens we need to talk about our real and raw feelings. We need to express our feelings to someone who cares enough to listen. I have friends who do this. They allow me to be real and to process the issues. They are people who listen and understand. God puts many people on the earth so that we can do this for each other. When someone lives out their role of being an understanding friend we can go to the next step. The next step is always getting our attitude right before God. God will always be the help we need to change us.

God is always the One who can pick up the pieces of a bruised soul and mind putting it back into the right perspective. I am glad I have friends who listen and let me vent my feelings but only God can fix me. When we decide to let God do His good work in our hearts we are choosing to love God enough to obey His directives. When we do this, we are changed bit by bit by bit (Philippians 1:6).

So, be a friend that people can share their hearts with in confidence. After being that friend then point people to the best Friend named Jesus who changes our weakness to strength and our wounding to comfort. This is what He does. As the song goes, "What a Friend we have in Jesus."

LINGERING in the LINES – Read Jeremiah 35

It's Personal

As I read the story in the Bible about God's people and their long 40-year travel in the desert I wonder about a few things (Exodus Chapter 14 - 17). What was more important to these people? Was it having food to eat in their hunger as God provided them with sweet bread from heaven? Or was it water to drink in their thirst as God provided it through the gush of water from a rock? Possibly it was shelter from the heat and wind as God provided that shelter with the home of tents and the covering of a cloud to block the sun. It well could have been the companionship with one another as they shared the experience of desert travel.

The most important thing could have been needing direction in what to do which God provided by selecting Moses as their leader. The most important thing could have been having clothes to wear which God caused never to wear out through their long desert travel.

Yet, as the story continues we find out that none of these things were of most importance. Despite all the provision God had given these people the Bible tells us they grumbled and complained. They demanded and sulked with "poor me" attitudes all through their 40-year desert journey. The most important thing to these people was not the God who provided them with His gifts of food, water, clothes, shelter, community, and leadership. The most important thing to these people was their self focused wants. Their self focus took away their ability to be satisfied and contented with God and His provision. Self focused wants should never be the most important thing in any of our lives. We will die in that desert. These people did.

LINGERING in the LINES – Read Hosea 14

Muscle Building

This verse in Daniel 10:18 says:
"Again the one who looked like a man
touched me and gave me strength."

The way to get spiritually strong in God is by having the Person who calls Himself Strength come and touch you (Psalm 28:7). The touch of strength comes to us as God speaks His Word to us. As we read God's Word and allow the words of God to sink deep into our hearts and minds we are revived. The words of God are for a reason. That reason is that you will be profoundly affected by them. In fact you will be so affected by God's words that it will change your viewpoint into God's viewpoint.

We are touched by God when we take His words with faith and apply God's words to our everyday life and its happenings. What is happening in your life right now that needs a touch of strength?

Have you lost a dear spouse? Then let God touch you and strengthen you with His words in Isaiah 54:5, *"For your Maker is your husband—the Lord Almighty is His name—the Holy One of Israel is your Redeemer; He is called the God of all the earth."*

Are you struggling with regret over past mistakes, sins and failings? Then let God touch you and strengthen you with His words in Isaiah 43:18-19, *"Forget the former things; see I am doing a new thing!"*

Are you struggling with emotions of feeling less then or inadequate? Then let God touch you and strengthen you with His words in Isaiah 43:4, *"You are precious and honoured in My sight and I love you."*

Are you struggling with loneliness? Then let God touch you and strengthen you with His words in Hebrews 13:5, *"Never will I leave you; never will I forsake you."*

Are you struggling with giving control over to God? Then let God touch you and strengthen you with His words in Isaiah 55:8, *"For your thoughts are not My thoughts, neither are your ways My ways"* declares the Lord.

Are you struggling with ruined things in your life? Then let God touch you and strengthen you with His words in Isaiah 51:3, *"The Lord will surely comfort Zion (His people) and will look with compassion on all her ruins; He will make her deserts like Eden, her wastelands like the garden of the Lord. Joy and gladness will be found in her, thanksgiving and the sound of singing."*

Let God strengthen you today with the touch of His words to your issues.

LINGERING in the LINES – Be open to God with your issues

Look! No Hands

God is God. He stands alone as the only One true God. That is what God says about Himself all through the Bible. In I Samuel of the Old Testament, God was symbolized by a tangible wood chest called the ark which contained God's presence. This ark had been captured by the enemy. The enemy had put the living true God into their temple beside their man made god statue named Dagon. In the morning the enemy went to their temple and found their god fallen over with its face to the ground. The next day the same thing happened only now the head and the hands were broken off of their man made god.

The living God never shares His Godhead with another or shakes the hands of the enemy. He stands alone as God. The living God is never in captivity. In fact, He came to set the captives free (Isaiah 61:1).

These things were happening in order for God to get the ark of God back to His people and out of enemy hands. When the ark was being sent around from one enemy house to another a strange illness was happening to the enemy. God was in essence telling the enemy that the place for God is in the hearts and minds of His people. This is the rightful place of God. God's perspective is that no enemy has the authority to keep God from coming to His people.

This story is God telling us that He wants people to regard Him as the One and only true God. God wants you to receive His truth and put it into your mind with knowledge, and into your heart with life application. God desires people to have no other gods in their lives.

LINGERING in the LINES – Read 2 Samuel 22

New Shoes

There comes a time when we need new shoes. The old ones have been well worn and walked with us many miles on the journey. When I bought my new shoes and put them on my feet I had to adjust to the newness of these shoes. It takes time to break in something new and feel the comfort of it.

This is how it is to learn new truths about God and His ways. We get very familiar with what we know. Then, all of a sudden a life curve hits us that we did not expect and we need to learn new things. Learning something new about God may not be so comfortable at first. Possibly you have believed that the blessings of God are something you can only see in a temporal way. The new thing is that God's blessings are often unseen things happening in the heart of a person as they face the issues of life. God is always good and that makes Him a blessing God in every circumstance regardless of how that circumstance looks to us.

Sometimes the blessing of God is showing us our wrong attitude. This revelation is new and may hurt but God's blessing is to direct us to a better way. The blessing of God is having His comfort and compassion come to our hearts when circumstances cause us hurt and sorrow. The blessing of God is forgiveness when we fail. The blessing of God is giving us a settled heart. The blessing of God is giving us peace when everything around us is in turmoil. These blessings may be unseen but they are deeply felt and experienced. Now that is real blessing!

LINGERING in the LINES – Read John 15

No Worries

Our daughter and her husband had just become new homeowners when we received this call on the phone. I quote, "The sewer is coming up the shower, there is water in the basement and the fence fell over with the last snowfall." This is called life. Jesus tells us not to worry. Jesus knew that adding worry to the long list of life issues would not help our situation. Jesus knew that worry would just be the start of another list of the unsettled emotions of disappointment, frustration, and fear.

Jesus told us not to worry about tomorrow because today has enough trouble for our emotions to handle. Jesus told us not to worry about what we will eat or wear because God knows our needs and long ago made provision for those needs. Jesus told us not to worry because He wanted peace for us instead of panic (Matthew 6).

Jesus told us not to worry because there is something we can do rather than worry. We can pray. We can call the plumber. We can go grocery shopping. We can fix the fence and we can buy the clothes we need. Pray and thank God that He supplies everything to meet your needs. Pray and thank God for creating you with the ability to work. Pray and thank God for the money to pay for the plumber, the food, and the clothes. Pray and thank God that He has given other people the abilities to fix the temporal things that break. Then, after you finish your thanksgiving prayers bend your knee to honour God who alone can mend your soul from worry to peace, from doubt to faith, and from fear to confidence.

LINGERING in the LINES – Read I John 5

Over and Over Again

There is a story in the Bible that Jesus tells us about prayer. There was a persistent widow who went to an unjust judge to get justice for an issue that she had been dealt unfairly with. The judge did not act on the matter and so the widow kept coming to him and repeating her request. Finally because he had heard her request so many times he granted it (Luke 18:1-8).

In this story we see one more picture of prayer as Jesus paints it. As we pray to God our prayers go up into the heavenly realm and in that realm there is a just God and an unjust enemy. The enemy wants to stop God from working on our behalf. The enemy tries to block prayer answers and in the delay we may get discouraged and give up. That is what the enemy wants us to do. We must be like this widow in the story and continue to pray ceaselessly until the situation has been dealt with. As we continue in persistent prayer against our unjust enemy he moves out of the way. Then the God of justice parts the heavens and comes down with the answer to our prayers.

Daniel in the Bible had prayed to God about a problem and God heard his prayer. But there was a war in heaven against the prayer of Daniel and it caused the answer to be delayed three weeks. It may have been delayed but the answer did come. So, take heart and keep praying for the enemy to move out of the way and you will see answers. God wants us to be persistent in prayer because God battles the enemy too.

LINGERING in the LINES – Read Psalm 136

A Bag, A Purse & A Sword

When Jesus was about to leave this earth and go back to Heaven He told His followers to get a purse, a bag and a sword. When He was with them they lacked nothing because they had Jesus pointing them to the way to do life. Take the resources of a "purse" or "money" that God has given you using that money to pay bills, buy food, give to the church, support missionaries, and to whatever areas God asks you to give to. Always remember that God is your Provider because that is His name.

Take the "bag" or your "life" with all your abilities, talents, and opportunities and use your life as an offering to God, to be used for His purposes. Be sure to remember that God is the Provider of your life. In remembering this you let God know that you want to share in the expansion of His kingdom here on Earth.

Take the "Sword" which is the Word of God using it to get to know God more and more. Remember that God is your Provider of all the truth that you will need to know how to live your life.

Jesus used all His resources to do the will of His Father and to help the world. Should we do any less?

LINGERING in the LINES – Read Luke 22

Practice, Practice, Practice

The speaker asked a question—Are you practicing the presence of God in your life or are you practicing the presence of problems? I thought that was an interesting question that deserved a moment of pondering. What does this all look like? Well, when was the last time you thought about your body and how it walks and talks and breathes with bones, muscles, hormones and organs? God made your body to function in a designed rhythm. God fashioned you. He is your Creator. Pondering this is practicing the presence of God.

When was the last time you really listened to a bird sing or watched the rustle of the trees? God made this. He is your Creator. Pondering this is practicing the presence of God. When was the last time you opened the Bible to read and absorb what God looks like in His words? God desires to speak to you through His words and God wants you to take notice and listen. This is practicing the presence of God.

Are you thinking about problems in your life? Are you wondering how the next bill will be paid or how the next doctor visit will go? Are you wondering how you can get through to your teenager or how you can keep joy in the routine? If you are thinking like this that is the practice of problems. Whatever we focus on in our minds and rehearse over and over again is called practicing. Let us choose to practice the right presence. When we choose to practice the presence of God the problems will not be our focus.

LINGERING in the LINES – Read Psalm 33

Show and Tell

When we read the Bible there may be times when things look like they are conflicting. But I can assure you they are not. They may seem conflicting because we need to do a deeper search to what God is telling us. Never doubt the accuracy of how God speaks through His Word. He will never make a mistake in what He says. We can trust God and His Word.

In Ecclesiastes 5:1-2 it says, *"Guard your steps when you go to the house of God. Go near to listen rather than offer the sacrifice of fools, who do not know what they do wrong. God is in heaven and you are on earth, so let your words be few."*

Then in Hosea 14:2 it says, *"Take words with you and return to the Lord."*

God speaks. He wants us to listen to His view about us in what we are doing and thinking. In listening we do not speak from our own voice. In listening we can hear what God is trying to tell us. There is a time to listen and there is a time to speak. When we understand the majesty of sitting in the presence of the King of kings we will choose to listen. When we stand in awe of the Creator of the world we will choose to listen. The God who is above all created things wants to talk with you. God wants to tell you many things so sit back and be still and allow His holy whisper to overshadow you with grace and truth (Jeremiah 33:3).

God also desires for us to take words with us. God wants to hear our voice and see our face (Song of Songs 2:14). God longs for us to trust Him with our words of repentance, struggles, joys, requests, and praise.

LINGERING in the LINES – Read Revelation 22

Smoke

I am sitting here on the front step of my home. I look up into the sky and I see a long white line of smoke. There is an airplane flying above my head but I cannot see it. All I can see is the sign the pilot is leaving behind his plane to let me know he is there. This unseen pilot is flying an unseen plane in the sky and yet I know he is there.

This unseen plane story speaks about our God. He is here. He is with us. An unseen God is moving and working among us, and we get to see what God is leaving behind. As God travels unseen into the chaotic issues of our lives I see the peace beyond understanding that God gives. As God travels unseen into the depressions and discouragements of our minds I see the hope of a renewed mind healed with joy that God gives. As God travels unseen into our fears of the future I see the courage that God gives us to move forward and conquer. As God travels unseen into the worries of today I see the contentment that God gives.

We have an unseen God who can be clearly seen by the evidence He leaves behind of who He is and what He can do (Hebrews 11:1). So never doubt that there is a God working in your life and all its issues. He is there, just look up!

LINGERING in the LINES – Read Colossians 1

Strategy of Hope

In Psalm 119:50 there is a verse that reads like this, *"My comfort in my suffering is this: Your promise God preserves my life."*

The fellow who wrote this really understood that the promises of God are the help we need. The promises of God help us because there is a living God behind those promises who is true to His word.

So what are some of God's promises that comfort us in the suffering issues of life? How about "I will never leave you or forsake you." Or "The Lord will watch over your coming and going both now and forevermore." Then there is "Is anything too hard for the Lord?" Another promise is "Be strong, do not fear; your God will come." How about the promise of "My God will meet all your needs according to His riches in Christ." Truly our comfort is in the promises of a promise keeping God. This is the abundant life which Jesus promised us when we walk confidently into His truthful presence.

Whatever you face today let it be known that God is with you. His watchful care is always designing a way to meet you in whatever place you sit, stand or walk. These promises of truth will be your strategy of hope the next time you find yourself suffering an issue of any kind.

LINGERING in the LINES – Check out a Bible concordance to find out where these listed promises are found and take time to read Psalm 111

The Bibles

Within a short span of four months I lost both my elderly parents. They were gone and what they left behind for me was their faith. I took their Bibles and walked through the pages with them as the cloud of witnesses that had gone before me. I saw the markings on the Bible pages of their journeys with God. As I read their notes in the Bible margins my own faith was ignited with a new flame. This flame reminds me to keep the fire of passion for God burning in my own life. It was their walk with God through His Word that inspires me to walk in the same truth that they did.

There never was any dust on the Bibles of my parents. They lived by the Word of God. They ate the book in application to their daily life and problems. They drank the book to keep hydrated from the world that offers no water to quench the thirsty soul. They loved the book because they loved the God of the book.

The Bibles of my parents were spread out on a kitchen table with a cup of coffee. There at that table they knew that God was God and there was no other (Isaiah 45:5).

Many people graced the hospitable home of my parents as they led Bible studies encouraging others to live by God's words. They made God their home and God made His home their home (John 14:23).

The legacy of faith in the words of God lives on and on and on for everyone who reads The Book and lives by it. So read on and leave a legacy for all who come behind you! You are the cloud of witnesses (Hebrews 12:1).

LINGERING in the LINES – Mark up your Bible and leave notes in it

The Decision

We make decisions every day about what we do or think. Sometimes those decisions can be beneficial to us or detrimental. One day Jesus was teaching His disciples about the future for them. He told them that they would come against all kinds of enemies in the days ahead. After Jesus finished telling them the difficult things that were going to happen He said this to them, *"But make up your mind not to worry beforehand how you will defend yourselves. For I will give you words and wisdom that none of your adversaries will be able to resist or contradict"* (Luke 21).

This is very important news for us today many years after Jesus expressed this encouragement. We all need to decide beforehand not to worry about issues and the people that contribute to our issues. This decision not to worry but to trust God is beneficial to us. Jesus told the disciples that He would give them the words and the wisdom to handle difficult things. When we make the decision beforehand to trust God and not worry we can be settled with a peace that transcends our human understanding in all of our life situations (Philippians 4). Peace is real!

LINGERING in the LINES – Read Job 39

The Favourites

I have so many Bible verses that stick with me and shape my life each and every day. These verses provide continual encouragement to me. I encourage you to make your own list of God's words that will stick with you.

Psalm 143:8
Let the morning bring me word of Your unfailing love, for I have put my trust in You. Show me the way I should go, for to You I lift up my soul.

Psalm 119:49
Remember Your word to your servant, for You have given me hope.

Psalm 105:4
Look to the Lord and His strength; seek his face always.

Psalm 86:3
Have mercy on me, O Lord, for I call to you all day long.

Psalm 73:25
Whom have I in heaven but You? And earth has nothing I desire besides You.

Psalm 73:28
But as for me it is good to be near God. I have made the Sovereign Lord my refuge; I will tell of all your deeds.

LINGERING in the LINES – Settle these verses into your mind and soul

Forever

We are fragile in our view of leaving all we see and know. There are so many unknowns that we get weak in the knees and feeble in our thoughts as we consider leaving this world of time as we view it through our eyes. Is it hard for us to settle our minds about this final passage?

It might help us to settle this issue when we realize that everything we see is a created work. It is arranged under the hand of God and it will never die. Artists paint and authors write. Cooks prepare feasts with delicious food. The farmers plant and speakers speak. Preachers preach and builders build. That is just how God arranged it all as the Creator. Everything we do is orchestrated by the original design of God. God will always be the Creator because that is who He is. God will never waste the creative work He has called people to do.

God is everything that He shows us to do. He is the Builder. He is the Gardener, the Vine, the Branch, and the Tree. God is the Author and Writer of the story. God prepares the food in the feast called the Bible. God is a speaker and an artist of renown. This is the God of the Bible. God set all of these creative works in place because they are eternal to God. This gives us a settled spirit to leave behind what we see in part to gain what we will see in the whole. Heaven will be that place. Let this forward look strengthen those weak knees and keep walking to your final destination. Let this forward look strengthen the feeble thoughts of your own into the mind of Christ that is in you (I Corinthians 2:16).

LINGERING in the LINES – Read Isaiah 35

What Do You See

Christmas is all about the sights, sounds and smells. In order for Christmas to be true to its name we need to see a baby. In this baby we see a massive God who owns the universe become so tiny that He fits into a small womb. We see the powerful hands of God forming His humanity in a womb that He created. In this baby we see the beating heart of God and with every beat we hear, "For God so loved the world He sent His Son."

In this baby we see the eyes of God as He watches over our coming and going both now and forevermore (Psalm 121). In this baby we see the mind of God who knows all things. In this baby we see the ears of a God who hears our cry and is attentive to our voice (Psalm 34). In this baby we see the blood needed to sustain physical life. This same blood is what we need to sustain spiritual and eternal life. One day long ago that blood was poured out for the whole world as the body of Christ hung on a cross. This holy blood cleans up our sins with forgiveness and salvation. In the words of an old Christmas carol I ask you, "Do you see what I see?" May Christmas always cause you to see this baby and know that He is God.

LINGERING in the LINES – Read Psalm 148

What God Is Not

The story Jesus told in Luke 18 was about a widow who was dealing with an injustice done to her by an adversary. Her situation was being handled by an unjust judge who did not fear God or care about people. The unjust judge would not listen to the plea of a widow until the annoyance of her persistent asking overwhelmed him. He was so weary of her asking that he granted her request. Justice had been done.

I believe God was telling this story so vividly so that we could easily see the distinction of the evil of man and the good of God. The unjust judge knew he did not fear God or care about people. He also knew that justice did not matter to him. Jesus is telling us here how different God is. God knows who He is and that His kingdom is all about caring for people with love. God hears His people and with great kindness responds to their prayers. God's righteousness cares about justice being done to the oppressed. God's mercy and compassion is not annoyed by our needs. God desires our constant entrance into His presence with ceaseless prayer. In fact He asks us to come.

Yet despite knowing God's character Jesus asks this question of each one of us, *"When the Son of Man comes, will He find faith on the earth?"* (Luke 18:8). God is reminding us to have faith in Him and His desire for justice. Faith is to believe God! So, let there be faith on the earth and let it begin with you.

LINGERING in the LINES – Read Luke 18

But As For Me

In the Bible we read stories of many real people who did right in the sight of God in a few situations but stopped doing the right thing over the continuance of their life. In 2 Chronicles 25:2 it says, *"King Amaziah did what was right in the eyes of the Lord, BUT not wholeheartedly."*

There is a difference between just following God and wholeheartedly following God. The difference is that following God is all about me and wholeheartedly following God is all about Him. God wants devoted love and not just going through the motions of doing the right things. I can prepare supper for my family with the drudgery thinking of I have to make supper. This would be following because it is the right thing to do. Then again I can prepare supper for my family with the attitude of I want to do this because I love God and my family. This would be wholeheartedly following God because I am doing everything as to the Lord for His view (Colossians 3:23).

King Amaziah's lack of wholehearted devotion caused him to eventually leave God. That is the apathy that happens when the following is just doing the right thing. The reward of following God for selfish purposes is lost purpose and lack of love in everything we do. The reward of following God with wholehearted devotion is to know love Divine so great and wondrous. This is the purpose of life that gives joyful meaning to everything we do. *In* Psalm 73:8 the Psalmist says, *"But as for me, it is good to be near God. I have made the Sovereign Lord my refuge."* May you make the declaration of "But as for me" for yourself and purpose to follow God wholeheartedly!

LINGERING in the LINES – Read Psalm 73

Find the Face

"Look to the Lord and His strength; seek His face always" (Psalm 105:4).

Whatever you are facing today you need the face of God to help you. When faced with the sorrow of loss you will need to see the face of God as Comforter. When faced with financial worries you will need to see the face of God as Provider. When faced with loneliness you need to see the face of an Ever Present God.

When faced with unanswered questions you will need to see the face of the All-Knowing God. When faced with a defeating circumstance you will need to see the face of God as Conqueror.

When faced with restlessness you will need to see the face of God as Prince of Peace. When faced with death you will need to see the face of God as the Resurrection and the Life. When you are faced with illness, wounds or hurts you will need to see the face of God as Healer.

When faced with a broken life of wrong choices you will need to see the face of God as Restorer and Rebuilder. When faced with obeying God you will need to see the face of a pleased God. When faced with personal rebellion or apathy towards God you will need to see the face of a grieving God. Find the face of God in every area of your life and in every situation and you will know God up close and personal!

LINGERING in the LINES – Read Psalm 136

Lamb, Mutton or Hogget

There are many different kinds of sheep. God has a reason for likening us to sheep. The lamb is a tender, very tender meat that is less than one year old. The mutton is a tough meat from a sheep over two years old. The hogget is meat that is neither tender nor tough and is from a sheep under two years old. God in the Bible often refers to His people as sheep. In light of the various kinds of sheep with their toughness or tenderness or lack of both I wonder which sheep are we?

Are we so tender to God that He can speak His love to us and guide us through the issues of our lives? The tender lambs are young and always see themselves in need of the Good Shepherd to shepherd them with His watchful care, guidance and protection. Are we so old in our knowledge of God that we have out grown our need to be dependent on leadership from the Good Shepherd? In this attitude we grow tough with the pride of closed eyes to see the path the Good Shepherd is leading us to. In this attitude we grow tough with the selfishness of closed ears to hear the Shepherd's call to go to higher places where there is more pasture to feed on.

Do we speak the Christian language so well, and yet fail to walk out that language in our actions because we are indifferent? This indifference is a lukewarm attitude of disregard to the Good Shepherd and His deep desire for people to come home to His heart.

We all need to take the time and ask ourselves what kind of sheep we are at this very moment in our lives. The answer will shape us each day as we regularly revisit our relationship with our Good Shepherd.

LINGERING in the LINES – Read Psalm 23 and read it slowly

Lead On

"The Lord is my Shepherd I shall not be in want. He makes me lie down in green pastures. He leads me beside quiet waters, He restores my soul. He guides me in paths of righteousness for His name's sake" (Psalm 23).

This familiar Psalm is read so often that I wonder if we take the time to linger in the lines to see the power of the Psalm for each of our lives.

When we allow the Good Shepherd to guide we will always be led into the good paths of God's right way to live. Most of the time our problem is not about being led but about who is leading us. When we allow temporal things like clothes, opinions of others, food, work, ministries, and other activities to lead us these become our shepherd. And this is not a good shepherd. This kind of leadership does not lead us into the right paths of a God directed way. It leads us into the misdirection and confusion of a self run or culture run life.

The Good Shepherd leads us into His heart where there is soul satisfaction and a settled spirit. The Good Shepherd leads us not to want people approval, prestige, affluence, and power. The Shepherd has the ability to satisfy all of our needs so we don't want things that ruin us. When the Shepherd leads us we are restored from the cycle of want. *"Surely goodness and mercy will follow us all the days of our lives and we will dwell in the house of the Lord forever."* This is a place of belonging called home and the Good Shepherd will lead us there.

LINGERING in the LINES – Read Isaiah 58 and let God lead you

Tripped by Truth

We live in a world with so many views it can make our minds and spirits spin with uncertainty and confusion. Life does not have to be lived that way. There is another way to live. God has given us His directive to follow and His Book is over flowing with truth and only truth. When God walked the earth as Christ He called Himself "The Truth"(John 14: 6). This declaration comes from the mouth of God who speaks no lies, and as a result of this declaration we can now know the truth (Hebrews 6:18).

When God tells us the truth it does not mean we are listening to His truth and applying it to our daily lives. When we do not want to listen to the truth then we stumble in it becoming confused and directionless.

Isaiah 59:14 says, *"So justice is driven back, and righteousness stands at a distance; truth has stumbled in the streets, honesty cannot enter."*

When we neglect God's truth it is driven away from us by our own choice. When we neglect God and His truth we are actually choosing to live our lives regarding lies and revering the evil one who is the author of lies. God told us to set no other gods before us. Living in the lies is putting lies as the god we serve and worship.

Let us not allow our tantalizing personal views to take precedence over the truth of God because if we do we will lose. We will lose our freedom, our joy, our purpose and we will lose God's sovereign all-knowing view as the plumb line for all we do and think. Don't stumble over truth and be lost in the lies. God has better plans for you than that!

LINGERING in the LINES – Read Isaiah 55

Wise Guy

Jesus told a story about ten people—five wise and five foolish. They were on a journey towards God with lamps or lives filled with the oil of views. The five wise people had the views of God as their compass of direction. The five foolish people had their own personal views or the views of culture as their compass. They were all heading in the same direction towards God yet only the wise ones would get into the place of the heart of God.

The only view that will ever get us into the eternal things of God is the view of God. This is the view of wisdom. Anything less will fall short regardless of how right it may seem to the human thoughts. This is the view of foolishness. In Isaiah 55:9 it tells us that God's ways and thoughts are higher than and above our ways and thoughts. The foolish people were sincere in their religion but sincerity is not enough when traveling towards the heart of God. We need to be on the road of God's truth because that is where God is. God calls this road a narrow road so that we stay real close to Him. The narrow road is a gift from God because it blocks the ease of veering off in a broader direction of conforming to the culture or living independently with self views (Matthew 7:14).

In all the time that the foolish were around the wise nothing about the very heart and truth of God had rubbed off into their lives. Foolishness is never humble enough to learn from the wisdom of the truth of God and His words. Foolishness asserts itself as the final answer to its issues. The definition of being foolish is having no wisdom.

LINGERING in the LINES – Read Matthew 25

The Nerve

Jesus said that if we hunger and thirst for righteousness we will be filled. In order to be filled we need to recognize we are empty. If we are empty with worry we need to be filled with God's perfect peace. If we are empty with agitation and frustration we need to be filled with God's daily joy. If we are empty with hate we need to be filled with God's continual forgiveness. If we are empty with loneliness we need to be filled with God's presence of friendship and belonging.

When we don't fill our emptiness with God there is a raw nerve that shoots pain into our souls. I liken it to a cavity in the tooth that needs filling. Until that tooth is filled there is a nerve pain that shoots through the jaw and the pain overwhelms us with its intensity. Once that tooth is filled the nerve is covered and the pain is released. The tooth is settled. This is so like our souls. When we fail to fill our lives with God and His righteousness we will remain an empty person with longings that pain the soul.

"Blessed are those who hunger and thirst for righteousness for they will be filled" (Matthew 5:6). So, let the hunger and thirst begin and you will know that God satisfies the soul. When you know what God can do let it spur you to believing what God will do and watch your life be filled to overflow. David in Psalm 23 said to God, *"You anoint my head with oil, my cup overflows."* Psalm 107:9 says, *"God satisfies the thirsty and fills the hungry with good things."*

LINGERING in the LINES – Set up a private communion with God of juice and bread

A New Step

I recall the day with clarity as I write this today. My son had not seen a personal God for his own life yet and as a believing mother I prayed for this boy. God impressed on my heart to give up meals for a 40-day period for my son. So all three of us, God, my son (unknown to him) and myself embarked on a journey forever impressed on all of our hearts.

As I was reading the Bible God gave me this word from His heart that assured me God was on the move with this son of mine. It is found in Isaiah 43:18-19, *"Forget the former things; do not dwell on the past. See, I am doing a new thing! Now it springs up; do you not perceive it?"*

God moved my son to read the book of Genesis in the Bible. As my son was reading the Bible he had an experience with the living God and His powerful and active Word (Hebrews 4:12). God became real to him in a personal way. I was on my way to the store and my son came running up from the basement stairs and I knew without a word that my son was a new person. This verse in 2 Corinthians 5:17 says it all, *"Therefore if anyone is in Christ, he is a new creation; the old has gone, the new has come!"*

My son was a brand new person who now had a relationship with the God who created him and called him by name (Isaiah 43:1).

"For God so loved the world that He gave His one and only Son, that whoever believes in Him shall not perish but have eternal life" (John 3:16).

My son was fully alive in his soul because the God who gives eternal life had come to him and was alive in my son. Let this same God speak to you as you walk through the pages of His Word and receive what He says to you.

LINGERING in the LINES – Read 2 Samuel 22

An Inside Job

We really can see and feel the changes around us. As I went off to work this morning there was a fall feeling in the air. I also saw how much darker it is now in the mornings because the summer season is about to change to fall. We not only see things happening around us but we feel it as well. We not only see things and feel things but we know things. We know through the course of history and the creation of things that seasonal changes happen. We know and we experience.

The Bible says that we can know God by the creation that surrounds us (Romans 1:20). We can see God and His activity because He is moving the wind about and rising the sun and growing the crops. We can plant and water all we like but if the Creator of all things doesn't make it grow it will not grow. I call this a dependent reverence. We need God. The sooner we realize this truth the happier we will live with purpose and meaning. When we decide to make an honest attempt to believe we need God then we will experience God's love. Who doesn't like to be believed in, you do. So does God. It shows value to you when people believe in you and it shows value to God as well.

We can know God and have knowledge about Him and His ways by tucking His Words into our hearts and minds. So tuck away and live in the wonder of the peace and hope of God no matter what happens around you. This is an inside job!

LINGERING in the LINES – Read Psalm 119

Drop a Knee

Abraham Lincoln, who was the 16th president of the United States once said, *"I have been driven many times to my knees by the overwhelming conviction that I had nowhere else to go."*

That should be our conviction as well. So today and every day drop a knee. They do it on the sports field and you can do it in your field of life.

A Prayer – "Dear Father in Heaven

I come to You because there is nowhere else to go. You know all the details about everything before it even happens. I come to You because You understand my sorrows, my failings, my longings and desires (Hebrews 2:18). I come to You because You have the power to move anything out of the way that is stopping Your good plans from being accomplished. I come to find grace, mercy, peace, comfort, understanding and direction. I pray Your Word from Psalm 32:8 over me, *"I will instruct you and teach you in the way you should go; I will counsel you and watch over you."* So, I come to be taught and instructed by you Lord, the brilliant Universe Builder. I come to You to receive Your counsel in what I should do and when. I come to hear Your voice speaking to me so that I can know Your will for me. I come to thank you for watching over me (Psalm 121). *In Jesus Name, the Name that leads me to the living God I pray AMEN."*

So drop a knee and pray a prayer!

LINGERING in the LINES – Read Isaiah 62

He's Gone, She's Gone

"And the Word become flesh and dwelt among us." This verse from the first chapter of John in the Bible speaks to us about Jesus coming to earth born in human likeness. God was doing life on earth just like us. God lived here so we could know that God understands what we go through as human beings.

Jesus who is called *"The Word"* desires to make His words become flesh to us or to become a reality in our day to day experiences. I recall the day my father died. I was overwhelmed with grief at this great loss in my life. As far as this earthly existence goes I would never see His face or hear His voice again in actuality.

After the funeral I sat alone with my Bible open on my lap. I happened to be reading in the book of Jeremiah 31:13 and suddenly this verse sprung off the pages and into my soul,

"Then maidens will dance and be glad, young men and old as well. I will turn their mourning into gladness; I will give them comfort and joy instead of sorrow."

God had taken away my sorrow and I was full of God's joy. This was God making His words real to me. God's joy had overcome my mourning. Then four months later my mother died and again the grief was overwhelming. I prayed and said to God that He had taken my mourning away at my father's death, and now would He do it again. God whispered to my soul *"I will."* And He did. "The Word" became flesh and dwelt among us." This is real!

LINGERING in the LINES – Read Jeremiah 31

Fear Be Gone

We live in a world with many issues and problems and yet we refuse to or don't realize we need to go to God for a strategy to help us get through.

God has a strategy for each and every situation of life even when the issues of our lives are a heavy weight in our soul. Possibly we just don't know how to navigate through God's Word to see the answers we need.

Ecclesiastes 8:5-6 says, *"This wise heart will know the proper time and procedure for there is a proper time and procedure for every matter, though a man's misery weighs heavily upon him."*

To know God's procedures we will need to read the Bible. If you read from a Bible reading plan you will be consistent in the strategy to get God's Word into your thinking. This is the way to gain the knowledge in order to know what to do. Then stop and reflect about what you have read.

Pray as you go asking God to show you His way to deal with your issue. God speaks in a way that you can know. It is an impression, it is a knowing and it is God. *"My sheep (My people) know My voice"* are the words of Jesus in John 10.

The declaration of Jesus is true and we need to affirm it in our lives by faith. We need to declare with our own mouth to believe everything God says. As you sense what God is saying to you then respond with obedience to what God is asking you to do.

Possibly you have a grudge towards someone and you are reading Matthew 6:14, *"For if you forgive men when they sin against you, your heavenly Father will also forgive you."* After you finished reading this verse, you will know that you need to let go of the grudge and forgive the offense so that you can be forgiven as well.

It may take some time to forgive but God understands the process. You just need to tell God that you are willing to forgive. God honours that desire. If you do not have the desire to obey God then ask God to give you that desire. He will do it. Jesus said that if you ask you will receive (Matthew 7:7-8). Then keep the goal in mind and walk towards the finish line of reaching that goal. Do not give up the good fight of faith. It will win over the natural bend of self. The victory comes from a conquering God whose own victories secure ours (Romans 8:37).

To do further study regarding an issue, get a concordance and look up all the listed verses on that particular topic. Then, read all those verses from God's Word and you will soon understand what you need to do to win over the issues of life. There is no fear here when life takes its blows on you because God has a strategy in how to conquer.

LINGERING in the LINES – Read Genesis 1

The Crown

My pastor said something that stayed with me. He said, *"Grow into your crown."* What does that mean for us and how is it accomplished? We have all come into a world of sin that has bowed its knee to every love except to a holy and righteous God. We cannot become right in our minds, attitudes and lifestyles on our own merits. We are imperfect people in need of a perfect God. The good news is that we have been given a gift by the hand of God and it is the righteousness of Christ. As we say "yes" to Christ in our lives He crowns us with Himself and with His righteousness (2 Corinthians 5:21).

Now that Jesus has given His righteousness to us we begin to grow into that crown. We grow into that crown as we apply God's ways and thoughts into our lives in obedience to God's Word. When God says, *"Do not fear"* (Isaiah 41:10) then we need to grow into the crown of faith and fear not. Every time you walk out in practical living the right ways of God you are growing into your crown. Jesus took the crown of thorns upon His own head so that we would not have to. His love took the ugly upon Himself and gave us the beauty. Now our obedience to God will be the crown of beauty we place on the head of Christ.

When we take our last breath here on earth it will have been worth it all! So grow away! One day you will place the crown of your life before the Throne of God and say to God, *"You are worthy to receive glory, honour and power, for You created all things"* (Revelation 4:10-11).

LINGERING in the LINES – Read Ephesians 6

The Dig

In the Bible, in Mark 4, God relates our souls to the soil, the seed and the harvest of a crop. Sometimes we live shallow lives and may not even know it. We may be trapped in our own views or in the desire to live by the culture and what it applauds. Sometimes we live under the sinister control of things like self exaltation, prestige, the love of money, worries, frustrations, or anger. This is not what we want to grow in our lives.

The way to change these things is to deepen the soil of your heart by going towards God and His deep truth. When you do this the seeds of God's truth replaces the shallow soil of a self or culture grown life. As you get into the words of God and believe those words you are deepening your life. In this depth the sinister control of the weeds of earthly things starts to lose their grip on you. As the weeds lose their place in the soil of your heart the planting of God's truth takes over and grows in the empty spots of your life. The new growth is good when we see peace grow instead of panic and love instead of resentment. These newly planted attitudes have roots that run deep because of the constant flow of the Living Water named Jesus.

The flourishing beauty in the garden of your life is now seen as the seed of kindness replaces the weed of rudeness and as the seed of gentleness replaces the weed of harshness. The seeds are endless and makes for a beautiful life as you watch your garden grow!

LINGERING in the LINES – Read Luke 8

No Fit

Several years ago my husband was changing into his jeans when he realized all too quickly that button would not reach the button hole. After several tries my husband could not understand why those jeans would not fit. As I sat down on the bed next to him to figure this out, I looked at the jeans and realized those were the jeans of our then 12 year old son.

When we try to live out a plan of life that is not the one we are designed to live things just don't fit. We become envious or jealous of the life that we see someone else living. We may even become hopeless when we see the lives of other people flourish when ours at times may seem like a desert experience. This kind of thinking just does not fit into what God wants for each one of us individually. Our selfish view always has a way of clouding the picture. When we focus on the God of our life we get less absorbed with what we don't have and what others do have. As we continually reorder our focus on God, we can see with clearer eyes the unique race that God has marked out for each one of us.

We need to throw off every heavy weight that keeps us from soaring with the life God has given us. We need to throw off the weights of jealousy, envy, insecurity, frustration, competitions, comparisons, and fear. If we don't throw off those attitudes and renew our mind in the truth of God we will never live the life God intends for us to live. Our destiny is to live by the truth of God's Word. When we do that we are in the right life and it fits!

LINGERING in the LINES – Read Hebrews 12

Poverty and Riches

When Jesus was a mere baby or small child a few wise men set out on a long journey to search for this new king. When they found Jesus they knelt and gave expensive gifts. Those gifts brought provision to the poverty of Jesus earthly parents. God promises to meet all of our needs and that is what God showed in this story. Mary and Joseph had needs and because of Jesus they experienced the provision to meet their needs. God has all kinds of ways to meet our needs even wise men from afar.

When we do the search effort and find this God born to us then we become rich in the provision God gives to us of hope, joy, peace, purpose, satisfaction, forgiveness, and life abundant. We are poor in these heart gifts unless God gives them to us. He alone has the exclusive rights to these gifts. *"And the Word became flesh and lived among us"* shows us God's desire to lavish these gifts on us (John 1:14).

The Bible says that all the promises of God are "yes" in Christ for each and every one who says "yes" to this King (2 Corinthians 1:20). Now it is our turn to lavish gifts on our beautiful Saviour. As we bow our knee to this King of kings may we offer God the gifts of our love, devotion, surrender, obedience, worship, and adoration. Let us offer these gifts to God with deep reverence and regard. He is worthy to receive all of our honour, glory, and praise.

LINGERING in the LINES – Read Luke 1 and Luke 2

He Did What?
We Did What?

Jesus came from heaven to earth.

"Today in the town of David a Saviour has been born to you. He is Christ the Lord. He will be great and will be called the Son of the Most High. For to us a child is born, to us a Son is given. For God so loved the world that He gave His Son" (Luke 2:11; Isaiah 9:6; John 3:16).

Jesus came to do this on earth.

"I have come that they may have life and have it to the full. The Son of Man came to seek and to save what was lost. Whoever comes to Me, I will never drive away" (John 10:10; Luke 19:10).

Jesus got this from the earth, from us, from humankind.

"I offered My back to those who beat Me, my cheeks, to those who pulled out My beard; I did not hide My face from mocking and spitting. All day long, I hold out My hands to an obstinate people who walk in ways that are not good. They continually provoke Me to my face. He came to His own but His own did not recognize Him or receive Him" (Isaiah 50:6; Isaiah 65:2-3; John 1:11).

God the Father did this to His Son after people did such evil to Him.

"Of the increase of Jesus government there will be no end. He will reign over His Kingdom, establishing and upholding it with justice and righteousness from this time on and forever." Because the Sovereign Lord helps Me, I will not be disgraced. I will not be put to shame. See My Christ will be lifted up and exalted" (Isaiah 9:7; Isaiah 50:7).

Thank you to Jesus for coming despite our actions to beat down the truth of God with our independent ways.

LINGERING in the LINES – Sing a Christmas Carol

The Garden Call

I never cared about the flower garden because whenever I would plant anything it rarely grew into anything lovely. The plants in the flower beds were always flowerless and small. One day as I was sitting on my front step of my home, I had a deep desire to develop a beautiful garden where the plants would grow and flourish. That desire was planted and birthed in me from God Himself. God was speaking to my soul to make this an adventure with Him. I the created one was experiencing the Creator. I needed to work in this garden in order to see the beauty.

I bought the plants. Then I plowed up the spot of earth before planting them. I watered, weeded and waited for God to grow the garden. It did take time and energy but all of a sudden there was a stunning array of colour, growth and beauty in the garden. All this happened because the Creator wanted to show me what could happen when God and people work together on a project.

The original garden that God created was called Eden and it was a beautiful garden. God asked the first born people named Adam and Eve to create with Him by caring for the garden. They were experiencing God. One day those caretakers of the garden stopped weeding the garden of their hearts. They listened to the sinister voice of the weed of their self views and let it grow clouding their vision of the beauty before them. They failed to water their lives with obedience to God and became flowerless and small. Don't let this happen to you. Let God create in you a clean heart because that is how the garden of the heart grows (Psalm 51:10).

LINGERING in the LINES – Read I John1:9

The Phone

I was comfortable with my old cell phone. I knew how to use it and I had become very familiar with it. When my phone renewal came up I was wondering if I should keep my old phone or step out into the new. I was anxious over even a little decision such as this. Finally, I let my yes be yes as it says in Matthew 5:37. Jesus says anything other than your yes or no in a situation is sin. I understand that because when we don't make a decision we get anxious, worried, and fearful which are sins to God. God tells us in His Word not to be afraid and not to worry (Isaiah 41:10). I always ask myself why we don't obey God because it is so freeing, settling and good for our lives.

So, I went forward with a yes to the new phone. It was hard to learn all the new things but eventually with a little help from my friends and perseverance I did learn. The new phone gave me the adventure of expanding my knowledge.

Sometimes we become so accustomed to our old familiar ways of doing things that we lose the adventure of the Christian life. Familiarity with God is not meant to remove adventure but to fuel us into new depths with God. Don't just stay content with what you know about God. You have a new plan which is to know *more* about God's character and His ways. God asks us to step out in faith so He can show us His power in fresh new ways. God is not a stagnant God but a God always working and on the move. So, move out with God and watch Him work.

LINGERING in the LINES – Step out in faith in an issue of your life

Search and Rescue

We are in a world of many people with many gods. We can know the One true God through the powerful and designed creation that is all around us. Yet, it seems that when we go through lonely or troubling times we wonder how this truth about God being the Creator can help us. Does God really care about us and what is happening? There was a man in the Bible named Job who was going through much pain and trouble. He lost his children, his possessions and health. The Bible records God speaking to Job about who He is and what we can trust when we are in the storms of life.

"Where were you when I laid the earth's foundation? Who marked off its dimensions? On what were its footings set, or who laid its cornerstone—while the morning stars sang together and all the angels shouted for joy? The earth takes shape like clay under a seal; can you bring forth the constellations in their season?" (Job 38).

God set up the earth shaping it with power, love and design. God causes the sun to rise, the moon to set, and the stars to shine despite all the disasters that come to earth. God shapes you in the same way. He will help you in the pain because God loves you. He will bring a good thing out of the pain because He has the power to design that (Romans 8:28). There is night and there is day. Only the Creator, the One and only true God can keep the things of earth sustained and He will sustain you. He is God.

LINGERING in the LINES – Read Job 38

Helpful, Healing, Holy & Hopeful

In Proverbs 25:11 it says that a word aptly spoken is like apples of gold in settings of silver. This is the way we need to speak to one another. Words aptly spoken breathe life to people. God breathes His Word into our souls and we live. He spoke into a dark formless world and it became beautiful with life. Ask yourself today if the words you speak are helpful, healing, holy, and hopeful.

We are in a world of words. Some words can wound, destroy, and control the soul. Other words can heal, build up, and free the soul. God's Word has threads of help, hope, healing, and holy love all through it. Every time God speaks His words life comes to us. God's Word will bring a needed correction into our lives healing us with the hope to change. God's Word will bring the comfort we need after a loss healing us with help to cope. God's Word is a word aptly spoken. God's Word is always apples of gold in settings of silver.

The holy words of help, healing, and hope are words that will leave a God approving legacy. This legacy will encourage another generation to do the same. Leave a legacy of valuable words with the sound of being aptly spoken. May the words of your life have the look of apples of gold in settings of silver.

LINGERING in the LINES – Give thought to the words you speak today

Messy Christmas

This was our Christmas. Our son's wedding was happening at an ocean resort. We had a flat tire on our car going to the airport. We missed a connecting flight due to a flight delay. We couldn't find our luggage to retrieve for the next flight. We walked more miles in the airport than I want to remember. We finally arrived in the city where the wedding was to be held. We were in the cab going to the resort when the cab had a flat tire. The driver did not have a jack so he attempted to lift the car with two large rocks that he found in the nearby ditch. The driver pulled the spare tire from the trunk only to realize that the spare tire was flat too. Finally, a friend of his arrived and took us the remaining miles to the resort.

The beautiful beach wedding was over and we headed home for Christmas. Our adult children arrived home for Christmas and brought their cats and their dog. Upon arriving at our house the dog thought the basement rug was a good bathroom and proceeded to make it such. The cat decided she ate too much and deposited those leftovers on the living room rug. Then the cats and the dog met each other and the meeting was messy, noisy and scary. There was hissing, barking, and jumping and that was not just the animals. But we had a great Christmas. I didn't buy a zoo but it felt like it. We were laughing and talking and in the end this was life at its best with the community of family. Just the way God planned.

LINGERING in the LINES – Relax and smile at a messy today

Character Matters

We need to grow in the knowledge of God in order to get strong in our souls. In Luke 2, it says that Jesus in His humanity grew and became strong in wisdom and favour with God and people. When God is in your life something should be happening to you. You should be growing strong in character. A person who desires this goal is wise indeed. Character is what you have at the end of the day. Jobs are lost, bodies age, crisis changes the world as we have known it, friends disappoint us, dreams die, and plans fail. When a person allows God to build His good character into them that person can weather the storms of life in confidence. We develop this confidence because God's truth and character are ruling our issues. God promises to give us a future and a hope and that is truly a confidence builder (Jeremiah 29:11). This confidence in God builds character.

As we grow in the knowledge of what God can do we grow in confidence to trust God's abilities. When God who is called Peace comes to our chaotic issues we experience God's peace. Then, as God develops His character of peace in us we can become peacemakers in the non peaceful issues that surround us. When God who is called Mercy comes to our wrongdoings we are forgiven and given hope. The wrong things we did will not destroy us. Then, as God develops His character of mercy in us we can be merciful to those that have wronged us. When we grow in character we are blessed by God because we look more like God looks. That is the look that changes our world!

LINGERING in the LINES – Do a character check on yourself

Mirth Month

Laughter is good for the soul. Joy is God's idea. The Bible is full of directives from God to be joyful always despite circumstances. There is always something we can look at with eyes of humour. For some people it takes a conscious effort to see the laughter in things. The beloved and late humour author Barbara Johnson was known for joy. She would tell us that it might take some digging but dig until you find the joy. Gratitude is linked to joy. It comes from your heart.

The soul of a person is where God makes Himself known. God helps us to apply all the good truth He has for us. God is constant and pure love in His character. I am thankful for this. God is open to hear our voice and open to talk to us about our lives. I am thankful for this. How about you? The truth is that if we start to be thankful for all the things of our lives we will be full of joy and laughter. Why do you think God would cause an almost 100 year old woman named Sarah to have a baby and to name him Isaac, which by the way means laughter, if God didn't know we needed to have joy and laughter in our souls. So laugh on!

LINGERING in the LINES – Watch a Ken Davis DVD

Perfectly Still

I sit in a lonely time today. How about you? Life has a way of laying us down from time to time. I turn my mind to wonder, to ponder, to question, to ask, and to receive. It is in these times that we need to get perspective on what we are experiencing.

Psalm 23 says that God makes us lie down in green pastures, leads us beside quiet waters, and restores our soul. This is the perspective. God is restoring our souls in the lonely times, in the broken times, in the sorrowing times, and in the empty times. God is in the continual process of restoring our souls. When we lay down in worry, loneliness or pain God moves us to the better place of dwelling in His Presence. This is the green pasture we should be lying down in. The pasture is green because in God's presence we are growing. We grow into a living relationship with Jesus because we are fed with God's truth. This truth helps us to live with the energy of God's perspective on all the issues of our lives.

Choose God's perspective and His life will flow in you. All of a sudden the loneliness is lifted by having a real living Person walking with you. The truth of God's Word restores your soul with the promise of God to never leave you or forsake you (Hebrews 13:5). This truth always settles down the lies that your emotions may tell you from time to time. All of a sudden your sorrow is lifted because the truth is God turns sorrow into joy to restore your soul. All of a sudden your worry is lifted because the truth is God is looking after you. He is looking after you and restoring your soul with His powerful ability to provide for your needs.

LINGERING in the LINES – Be still

God's World - Planted to Grow

The kingdom of God comes to us as a Seed (Galatians 3) entering our humanity. His name is Jesus. When we plant this good God into our souls we grow a large life. This life is large because we grow the plants of loving one another, forgiving one another, and helping one another. This is the large life that Jesus showed when He walked the earth. The Seed of Christ is showing us how to make a garden grow.

The Seed grows strong and healthy in us when the hard soil of anger, frustration and resentment and other hardening attitudes are plowed up. These attitudes are plowed up or overturned with God's gardening tools of wisdom, insight, personal revelation, truth, and circumstances. The soil of our hearts stays soft with our tools of surrender, commitment, and obedience to the will of God.

As the soil is plowed the softness of soul allows for the planting of new attitudes to take over and flourish and grow. The growing produces a large life where we get to rest in the shade of a God designed life. As we allow the continual planting of God's truth into our lives the weeds of selfish plantings are removed and the garden grows. Live the large life!

LINGERING in the LINES – Plant God's design in your attitude today

Stories

Everyone has a story. The Bible is full of stories. These stories are of real people and events and we learn from them all. Your story is a legacy left for people to learn from as well. When we have an issue in our lives the recovery stories of another help us in our own healing.

Paul was a recovering religious abuser. Eve was a recovering control freak. Peter was a recovering people pleaser. Matthew was a recovering money swindler. Elijah was recovering from an emotional collapse. David was recovering from a moral collapse. Abigail was recovering from a disappointing marriage.

All of these stories breathe of what God can do to redeem our mistakes and disappointments redefining our lives with healing and wholeness. All of these stories breathe of the faithfulness, mercy, and kindness of God. All of these stories breathe of the ability of God to rebuild and restore broken lives.

Share your story and help another in their recovery.

LINGERING in the LINES – Do a search of these people in the Bible

A Sweet Sound

God tells us to rejoice with those that rejoice (Romans 12:15). Why is it that we mourn fairly easy with those that mourn but we have a tough time rejoicing with those that rejoice? Why is it when someone is progressing well with great things happening in their life we are not thrilled for them? I believe there may be many aspects to this problem of the human soul. We may be so insecure in our own life plans that we can't appreciate when another is secure. Or possibly we have never been affirmed in the way we longed for so we can't get it over our tongue to say good things to others. How can this change? Our certainty and security will always be in a Person and never a thing. The only Person who is always there and never changes is the God of the Bible (James 1:17).

When we get the true picture of God and not the distorted view that so many live by, we will see that God has plans to give each one of us a future and a hope (Jeremiah 29:11). This truth makes it possible for us to rejoice in the future of another. God loves YOU personally and He has ordered a future for YOU. You never need to worry or be afraid or feel insecure over the success of someone else because God is involved with YOU. God has success for YOU as well as for another. There is no person that is embraced more by God than another. God's love shows no favouritism (Ephesians 6:9). So, now that you know the truth you can rejoice over others and their accomplishments with a sweet song and not a sour tune.

LINGERING in the LINES – Give genuine praise to someone

A Time to Cry

There is a story in the Bible that Jesus told as recorded in Luke 7. Jesus was invited to the home of a religious man. This man did nothing to show Jesus that He was a significant, appreciated or respected visitor to his home. As the evening progressed an uninvited guest arrived at the home. She made her way towards the Jesus she knew. Jesus had come to her with love and compassion and changed her life with hope, healing and forgiveness. She stood behind Jesus weeping at His feet with grateful tears for all God had done for her.

Her tears were so many that she wiped the feet of Christ with her hair to dry them. Not only did she cry tears but she honoured Jesus by pouring expensive perfume on His feet and kissing His feet. She stood behind the Jesus she revered as a symbol to acknowledge that Jesus would always be in front of her life as her honoured, regarded, and appreciated Lord.

She choose the feet of Jesus to pay tribute because she was so humbled that the Creator of all things would see her helpless estate and forgive her sins. She was humbled that God would restore her to the dignity that a sinful life had taken away from her. As this story of the Bible unfolds before our reading eyes and comprehending minds I wonder whom do you resonate with?

Are we the religious one content to be our own lord with our version of holiness? Or are we the one who knows there is no holiness in us apart from the Jesus who gives us His own? (Philippians 3:9).

LINGERING in the LINES – Take a moment and decide

God On The Shelf

I find it interesting that we do so many things that are required of us and never question the need to do them. For example, regardless of how cold it is outside we go to work. No matter how tired we are we make supper, clean the house, put gas in the car, and fix the broken heater in the garage and a multitude of other life tasks. This is normal activity for our lives to keep them moving forward.

Yet, when it comes to knowing God, living by His design and getting involved in the things that concern God we are too busy, too cold, and too tired. Why is that? God is the essence of our lives. He is the breath we breathe and yet this is how we treat Him. Could it be that we are putting off the urgent for the necessary?

My heartfelt suggestion to us all is that we attend the Bible study regardless of how cold it is outside. I suggest we read God's Book no matter how tired we are. I suggest we pray about everything no matter how many other things need to be done. For a Christian this is the normal activity to keep our lives going forward. When did we decide to do the things God desires for us IF we have time? How about making "Today God Is First" as our motto and then fit in the other duties as need be? Could it work? Try it and taste and see that the Lord is good (Psalm 34:8).

LINGERING in the LINES – Post "Today God Is First" on your fridge

Blurry Vision

Self esteem issues of feeling less than or somehow not enough are always flowing from a root of comparing ourselves to other people. When we do this the focus is me, always me. In order to get through this issue we will need to change our focus. The Bible tells us to fix our eyes on Jesus thereby making Him our focus (Hebrews 12:2). It is with this focus that we will start to see as God sees. God tells us to put our eyes on eternal things and not on earthly things (2 Corinthians 4:18 and Colossians 3:2). The reason for this is because God knows that when our eyes are on Him they are off of us.

Isaiah 57:2 says that Jesus in His humanity had no beauty that we would be attracted to. Yet in Psalm 27:4 David tells us that all he wants to do is gaze at the beauty of the Lord. David says this because in the eternal Godhead of godly character there is no end to the beauty of Christ who is called beautiful branch (Isaiah 4:2). This is the inside beauty of godly character that is seen far above the earthly human physical structure of a person.

When we fix on the development of the character of Christ in our souls then Jesus can do what He came to do. He came to bring beauty to the soul replacing the ashes of the earthly leanings of "all about me." When we fix on the eternal our self esteem soars with a God centered life. That is the only focus that will keep away the earthly low self esteem that is called "all about me." Let us purpose to think on the eternal just for today. Then just maybe you can think the same way tomorrow and the day after that.

LINGERING IN THE LINES – From the Bible read all the verses listed

Choose Not To

When you accepted Jesus as your personal Saviour and made a relationship with God your lifestyle you made a choice. You made a choice to give up the right to run your own life. You made a choice to allow God to take ownership of your time, agenda, desires, and resources. You made a choice to include God in every decision and plan. You made a choice to desire God's will above your own will. This is what having a personal friendship with God is about. I think that from time to time we may forget what our walk with God is supposed to be. This small writing is just a reminder to us all.

Sometimes we may wonder if God can run our lives better than we can. It is at those times that we start to take the reins of leadership back into our own hands. As we do this the attitudes of our heart start to unravel fairly quickly. All of a sudden our joy is gone. All of a sudden our peace turns into frustration. All of a sudden there is no awe of God but a drudgery to do life. All of a sudden we resent people and their demands on our time and energy. All of a sudden running our own lives doesn't look so good anymore. All of a sudden it happens.

Jesus has the government on His shoulders means that Jesus carries the government or the running of our lives as His responsibility (Isaiah 9:6). This is release for us because God is in control. God holds the universe in place by the laws He created. God holds you in place by the laws of His Word of instruction He created. Today allow God is rightful place in your life. Choose not to choose your own way!

LINGERING in the LINES – Release an issue to God today

Committed Security

We are never really secure when we worry and wonder if relationships are strong enough to hold. We will be on the edge most of the time with this kind of insecurity. We will display possessiveness, fear, anger, and a multitude of other emotions in an unhealthy way. We are not meant for this kind of insecurity. Jesus changed all that when He came and committed Himself to us in a personal relationship. This is a secure position of God with His people. He is All Powerful and can keep this relationship strong. He is true to His promises and will keep them. It is His unfailing and unending love that holds us to Himself (Deuteronomy 7:9; Isaiah 54:10).

God is called Freedom Giver and Prison Releaser so we never have to be chained with negative emotions that hurt our souls, bodies, and minds. Living in the security of this eternal relationship with God will help us in our secondary relationships with one another. When we live in the security of Christ we can offer the other people in our lives more love, grace, forgiveness, kindness, and mercy. We can do this because we are secure. We have nothing to lose!

LINGERING in the LINES – Make a loved one their favourite meal

Finish Well

Jonah was a prophet, meaning that he was a man of God, with an assignment from God. Jonah ran away from his assignment to tell the people that their ways of living were destroying them. Jonah was to tell the people that God had a better way for them to live. Jesus was different though. Jesus never ran away from His assignment of making us right with God and showing us a better way to live. As Jonah left God in disobedience his environment became quite stormy. As Jesus left His Father in heaven out of obedience His presence calmed the storms.

Jonah caught the next boat in order to get away. A fierce storm was happening because of Jonah's disobedience and it was risking the lives of others. Jonah told the owners of the boat to throw him into the sea and God would quiet the storm. They did that and the storm of the atmosphere settled. But the storm of Jonah's disobedient heart struggled nearly drowning in the depths of the sea. Jonah cried out to God to help. God answered his prayer saving him from death.

Jonah did eventually do what God desired him to do by preaching God's truth to a city that loved evil. The message of God that was delivered by Jonah moved the people to respond to God's love and mercy. Their hearts were changed to love God. Jonah hated these people for all the evil they had done. Jonah also hated that God offered these people love, mercy, and kindness.

Jonah lived the rest of his life in anger, bitterness, and resentment because he forgot how merciful and loving God had been in rescuing him. Remember that God's love for you is the same love God has for the whole world.

LINGERING in the LINES – Don't finish life like Jonah

Desert Beauty
(Based on Matthew Chapters 3 & 4)

I am going on a journey towards the heart of God. For this trip I have the ticket I need as I open up the Bible. I can now settle back into the seat of God's character. As I travel via "The Way" I will be brought to exceptional travel experiences of never to be forgotten places and people. I am thankful I am not doing this journey alone because you, who are reading this are my traveling companions. This trip will be bumpy, rocky, settled, and scenic for God really is in all of life. He is in the waiting on the runway, in the soaring in the skies, and in the walking on the path.

Here I sit and read about Jesus having a great moment when the sky rang out an affirmation from His Father who is in heaven. These positives words *"This is My Son, whom I love; with Him I am well pleased"* rang through the atmosphere to the earth and into the ears of the people and into the heart of Christ. The trip was going quite well. Then, all of a sudden Jesus was walking through a dry desert of the twists and turns of the tempting ways of the evil one.

In this culture driven world you will always be tempted with filling yourself up with anything and everything except God. Jesus didn't fall for that lie that twists the truth. Jesus knew that only with the words of God as His view and living out those words would He win. This is the only way we will win as well. Success is not what we see outwardly but what is happening in the inner soul. Jesus did not want temptation to defeat or define Him. He chose the ascension of victory and so can you!

LINGERING in the LINES – Speak God's Word into your issue

Eden or Not?

God made a flourishing Eden rich with communication and community of God and people. It was Eden because God was able to provide everything that His creation needed to flourish. Eve exchanged flourishing for languishing. Eve had a pursuit to be independent from God and that pursuit was spurred on by the evil tempter of every soul. Culture will ask you to fit in as it says to. The culture will try to redesign you to anything and everything as it sees fit to do so. Don't allow this to be the god you listen to. God says to be the "you" that He thought up for your life. God created you and so He knows better than anyone what you are meant to be. God is asking you to allow His voice to direct your views and choices.

There is only one true God (John 17:3) and He is the only one whose view will bring life and life abundant to you. Let God's plan for you be the measure to view your life from. His idea of you is the right idea. There will be no confusion when you allow your Creator to do His good work in your life. God is pleased when we consult Him with our plans. When you make it a life goal to please God you will never live a languishing life. Allow God to be the God in your life so that you will live a soul flourishing life full of adventure, expectation and intrigue. Regardless of how strong the temptation is we will never flourish when we choose independence from God. You or culture may think a self run life is Eden but it is not. It will turn out to be a barren desert of disappointment and regret. Let the God of all creation make your life an Eden delight as you depend on His resources to flourish.

LINGERING in the LINES – Check your view point

Enjoy You

When my mother was 88 years old her health declined and she needed to move to a personal care home. This was a big adjustment as are many things we encounter as we age. On one of my visits to her, I asked her how things were going despite all the difficulties that aging seems to bring. She said to me, "I am having a good time with myself." The declaration told me that regardless of the issues in our lives we are rich when we are filled with contentment. My mother had spent a lifetime learning to be content and then the day came when that developed character really mattered.

May we start today to learn and develop the "I am having a good time with myself" contented attitude. May we see the command of Jesus to love ourselves as one of the truths needed to do our lives well. God is delighted when we love ourselves because that shows God we love, honour, and respect what He has done in creating us. This is not selfish love but the strong healthy love that allows us to love God and others. When you have a good time with yourself then God and others will have a good time with you too. This is a powerful step to a meaningful life.

Are you having a good time with yourself? Here are a few suggestions. Sit in a café. Read. Be thankful. Pray Don't worry. Be positive. Enjoy your work. Savour your lunch. Embrace the quiet. Learn from the sorrow. Do it now because it does matter.

LINGERING in the LINES – Implement the above suggestions

Fresh Daily

There was a spiritual activity that was done in the Old Testament when yesterday's bread was removed before the Lord and replaced by freshly baked hot bread (I Samuel 21:6). God is showing us that we need a fresh visit from God each new day. God is a daily God. He wants us to see Him fresh, new, and hot every day. He doesn't want us to live on yesterday's activity but He wants us to live this day to its fullest. When we are hungry for God He will fill our souls with the bread of His Presence. This is what the Bread of Life does.

If we are hungry for this freshly baked hot bread, simply pray *"Our Father in heaven, give us today our daily bread"* (Matthew 6:11). God answers prayer. He Himself will come and make Himself known to you and fill you with His truth. Psalm 107:9 says that God fills the hungry with good things.

We need a fresh visit from God every day in order to handle the issues of this day. We need fresh hot new joy every day. We need fresh hot new peace every day. We need a fresh hot new hope every day. We will always need a daily perspective from God's view in all of our life issues.

LINGERING in the LINES – Read from a Daily Bible so that each day is covered with hot daily truth

Freedom Lovers

I simply love the truth, the principle and the word called redemption. In this life there is no one who has not done or thought something they regret (Romans 3:23). Often we believe the lie that there is no hope in our issues. The truth is that with God all things are possible. All things are not possible with us despite what the world view may be whispering into our ears (Mark 10:27). Why is it so hard to believe that the universe Maker can do all things? You see, despite regrets, failings, flaws, and bad decisions there is a God who tells us to put everything into His hands. Then, we are asked by God to watch Him work. This is how we will get into belief of God and know it is God. Jesus calls Himself the Redeemer. This is redemption (Romans 3:24).

Redemption really means deliverance through a price. Jesus took the hit with a nail to redeem all your issues and has set you free of self condemnation. You are free! Only when you give your life into the hands and heart of God can you experience this truth and shed the lie that He is not who He says He is. Your Redeemer will stand on the earth of your life issues and do a new thing in your life. Believe it (Job 19:25).

LINGERING in the LINES – Memorize Job 19:25

Question Period

Recently I decided to go into the Bible to see what kind of questions God is asking us. Questions are to make us think so that we can respond with an answer. God is asking us:

"Why do you call me Lord, Lord and not do what I say?" (Luke 6:46)

"Why do you doubt?" (Matthew 14:31)

"Where is your faith?" (Luke 8:25)

"Can you by worrying add a single hour to your life?" (Matthew 6:27)

"What do you want Me to do for you?" (Matthew 20:32)

The answers we give to God will determine how much we really believe about God. If we really believe that God is all powerful then we need to ask ourselves why we doubt that God can help us with our issues. If we really believe that God's Word is the truth then we need to ask ourselves why we don't live by God's words.

The next time you have a question for God remember that His question and declaration to you is, *"Do you love Me? Those who love Me will obey Me and abide in Me" (John 20:17; John 14:23).* Really, it gets that simple and yet that deep with God. Keep your heart tight with God! He loves you!

LINGERING in the LINES – Read John 21

Good God

We have a God who gives us amazing opportunities and the resources to do life well. God is patient and loving with us. He gives us repeated chances to do something good with what He has given us. God has a plan for each one of us. But if we are not careful the pride of life and independence from God's ways will cause us to ruin the good things God has in store for us.

The man in the story of Luke 16 knew that he was going to lose his job as a financial manager due to his unethical work on behalf of his employer. He reduced the debt his friends owed his boss which made the friends happy and secured friendships. This scheme did however cheat the boss out of his rightful money and severed the relationship with his employer.

God gave commendation to this man for the good principle to know he needed provision and doing something to ensure it. What God did not commend was the way the man accomplished it. God commends this principle of knowing we need provision because God wants us to ask Him for our daily needs. This asking ensures our dependence on God. When we don't live this way we cheat God out of His rightful place as Provider. What God does not commend or want from us is to find our provisions in anything other than God. We are not to look to people to give us our security. We are to look to God. This is the friendship we need to secure.

We may lose our jobs, influence, health, and even our friends but we will never lose the God who promises to meet all of our needs (Philippians 4:19).

LINGERING in the LINES – Ask God for your needs today

I Don't Like This

You will come across situations, relationships, and jobs you do not like. You will feel discouraged. You will. What are you going to do with that? Are you going to give up or are you going to deal with what you are facing? The choice is up to you. The choices you make will profoundly affect your life. So think about your choices and make ones that will bring life to you and not death. Think before you act on your impulses. If you don't feel like working get out there and go to your job. If you don't feel like loving a person just go and do a loving act for them. If you don't feel like finishing a project just go out and finish it.

Sometimes choices are tough because the good choice might require something from us that we do not want to do. It is not always about what we want to do but about what is the right thing to do. Each one of us needs to make our own lives work. We cannot expect another person to live our life. We must live it. Whatever good choice needs to be made in your situation, relationships, or jobs please make it. Making good choices by the design of God is the good life. God's good way of perseverance and endurance is what builds the character that will make God choices all along the journey of life.

LINGERING in the LINES – Read Proverbs 10

I Have Finished the Race

My daughter had signed me up to run a ten kilometer relay race for a shared experience. As I write this, the race is over and I finished it. I was straining for the goal ahead and I kept the faith that I would reach the finish line still running. I did not look to the other runners because they had their journey and I had mine.

As I approached the first bend in the road I told the fellow monitoring the runners' progress that I hadn't signed up for this but here I was. At the next bend in the race I was given an energy drink and cool water. I asked the attendant if it was reasonable for a 54 year old woman to run a race like this. He smiled and said, "You can do it, you're looking good." I had supportive praying friends with one friend promising to pray for me every fifteen minutes as I ran. We are all called to run either in the activity of an event, in the activity of prayer or in the activity of encouraging one another along the way.

This life is your run with God. Don't compare to other runners with wanting to be better than everyone else. Make it your goal to run your personal best for God. There will be things that will come to you in this life that you did not sign up for. To handle those issues well you will need the energy drink of seeing things from God's view. You will need the cool water of prayer and the perseverance of faith. Let's not forget that we will need a little help from our friends to encourage us to finish well. Run with God and finish well! You can do it, you're looking good and I am praying for you!

LINGERING in the LINES – Pray and encourage in the run called life

I Miss the Face

I just left the spot where they lowered my father to the earth where his face will be hidden for a time. I miss the face of faith in that man. I miss the face of love in that man. I miss the face of joy and adventure in that man. I miss the face of hope in that man. I miss the tears of that face. I miss it all. But I will see that face again. Again I will see the alive and enthusiastic face I have come to know and love. Again I will see the joyful face of a man who stood at the crossroads and looked for the ancient paths and chose the good path and walked on it (Jeremiah 6:16). Once again I will see the man that confessed with his mouth that Jesus is Lord and believed in his heart that God raised Christ from the dead (Romans 10:9).

Now, I tuck away into my memory everything I experienced with my Dad. This reminds me that we need to remember all the benefits God has given to us in our experiences with Him. What are your experiences with God? Spend some time remembering those things for the purpose of honouring your God. Honour your God with your gift of never ever forgetting the goodness of God's personality and His work in your life. The effort to do this will build your love for God as you keep walking on the good path.

LINGERING in the LINES – Remember the love of God & honour the memory of a loved one

In and Out of Season

One day as Jesus walked the earth with His disciples He was hungry. He saw a fig tree in the distance and wanted to eat of its figs. But when Jesus looked at the tree it had no fruit. Then Jesus caused the tree to shrivel up and He declared that never again would anyone eat fruit from this tree. Why such a strong word for a tree that was not even in the season to produce figs? (Matthew 21:18-20).

Jesus is making a spiritual point here for all of us to heed. We are God's workmanship and that means we are called by the God who feeds us to feed others (Ephesians 2:10). God is always in season with His truth. Regardless of our circumstances or our mood God wants us to be ready to tell anyone that comes to us about God. This is the will of God and is always in season. There are always people that need the food of God. There are always people that need to know that when they are weak God is their strength. They can feed on this truth and have their hunger satisfied. There are always people that need to know that God is with them in their loneliness and will never leave them.

Jesus told us to eat of Him, His views, and His truths. Jesus is always in the season to feed us because that is what He does. When you are in the season of planning your schedule please leave a spot open for anyone that needs a word from God through you. Be available for God to bring the fruit from the pantry of your life into the pantry of another life all season long!

LINGERING in the LINES – Schedule God into today's plans

Blooming Flowers

After my mother died one spring a wonderful couple named Gene and Alice gave me a set of pansies to plant in my garden. This was to be a visual remembrance for that summer. I planted those little flowers and they bloomed all through the summer. Every time I looked at them I thought of my mother. Early snow came that year and I did not get the time for the fall clean up of the garden. The winter was harsh and the snowfall very heavy that year. Spring did eventually come and as the snow melted I saw these little pansies with a full bloom of flowers facing me. They never died. Even though it was still quite cold these little flowers were shining in full form. I was amazed.

The appearance of those flowers was a visual love shown to me by God. God was telling me that on this the one year mark of my mother's earthly death she was alive and flourishing. Mother was with the Resurrection and the Life and she was as much alive as ever. Jesus came to bring life and told us that if we believe in Him we will never die even though we die (John 11:25).

Life is a gift given as a promise from God. God sees you with such value that He never wants you to be anything but alive, fully alive in His presence. God is not dead and neither are we who call Him Lord of lords, King of kings, Saviour, and Friend. My mother called God by all of these names and she lives on. She believed it when Jesus told her, *"I am the Resurrection and the Life, whoever believes in Me will never die even though they die."* She believed. May this be your story as well.

LINGERING in the LINES – Plant a flower in memory of a beloved one

Four Hour Prayer

Our church was holding a prayer week and I signed up to do four hours in the wee hours of the morning. As I signed up I asked a friend if she would join me in this adventure with God. I realized this would be a journey to stay alert and awake for God. God tells us in His Word how He never sleeps or slumbers so I was driven to give God a gift of wakefulness for this short period of time (Psalm 121).

I needed a way to navigate this adventure with success so I asked God for a prayer plan and He gave me one. I called it "A Plan 4 Purpose." Each hour would be a different topic that began with the letter P - people, places, projects and pastors. Every hour included the 3 W's - *worship* God by thanking Him for His character, *wait* on God for His thoughts on the needs to pray for and the actual *words* of praying for the issues.

I challenge you to do a prayer adventure with God. Call a friend and give God a gift of caring for His world as He does. Jesus loved adventure in life and in prayer. It is recorded in God's Word that Jesus walked on water, calmed a deadly storm, and cooked for 5,000 with only two ingredients of two fish and five loaves of bread (John 6). Jesus loved adventure and so can you!

LINGERING in the LINES – Sign up to pray

Invitations from God

I am impressed with God. He never forces or coerces or pins you to the wall with His truth and plan. *He invites* you. He tells you what He is all about and then *He invites* you to experience Him.

God invites us to wait, to pray, to weep, to heal, to forgive, to remember, to repent, and to love. *God invites* us to help ourselves with His life. *God invites* us to sit at His table and eat with Him. I love that generous nature and character of God. *He invites* us to His complete life. You get His mind. You get His unfailing love. You get His peace. You get His joy. You get eternal life. You get it all! Don't let this invitation go. I suggest we all reply with our "yes" to God.

After you say the "yes" you start on a forever journey to get to know God. He is the Author and Finisher of your faith (Hebrews 12:2). He wrote your story long before you were ever born. He pioneered the unplowed soil of your heart getting it ready to plant His invitation of love. God brings you through all kinds of life experiences to show you how faith in God works. One day God will finish His good work in you. God will then welcome you to your final and real home.

LINGERING in the LINES – Take one day at a time

It's Dead

I looked at the plant and realized it was gone. The sun was very hot and the root was too shallow to sustain its growth. I decided to replace the plant but I would wait until the next spring to do so. The next spring I went out to replant. As I looked at the spot where the dead plant was I saw a green shoot coming from the spot. There was life. I thought it was dead.

God plants Himself into our life and we become spiritually alive. God comes into us and begins to live His character of love, mercy, kindness, peace, and goodness into our lives. There will be times when we will not act in the character of God. We may act out of our own character of selfishness. We may hold grudges. We may act out of our own character of worry and fear. In these times it may look like the God in us is dead. But God is not dead. He is alive. He is called by the names the Resurrection and the Life (John 11:25).

The season for growing out of our own character and into the character of God is anytime when we allow God access to our grudges, anxieties, and fears. God is alive. He wants to grow Himself in you in all the seasons of your life. God is an all season God. Let Him grow.

LINGERING in the LINES – Look for the growth of God in you

It's a Holiday?

It was a holiday long weekend. We arranged for a flight to bring our son and his wife home for a vacation. Then we placed a call to our other adult children and they came home as well. Our yard was empty as the last of thirty year old rotting trees were removed from our yard. I missed the trees and longed to see beauty again. It was decided that we would plant a flower garden to fill this now barren land. The work began. The old grass was dug up and the old stones removed with a borrowed wheelbarrow from our neighbour.

The weather was cold and the rain relentless. Yet the family worked together. Holes were dug as shrub after shrub was planted hour after hour. Their backs were bent low to an unforgiving hard soil. The cold continued and hot chocolate was made and lasagna was baked giving inner warmth. Something new was happening. A new creation was unfolding.

Conversation was constant and laughter abundant. Everyone was home! This was family! This was love! The work was now done and the beauty was seen. This is the look of heaven. In heaven the conversation will be constant and the laughter abundant. The work will be done and the beauty will be seen. A new creation will have unfolded. Everyone will be home! This will be family! This will be love! Backs will be bent low in praise and honour to a forgiving tender God. Home at last! This will be heaven!

LINGERING in the LINES – Do a family project together

So Good

When you head home tonight you will see a sunset. As you look up into the night sky you will see stars. When you arise early you will see a sunrise. As you go through your day you will see the sun or clouds. You will hear birds and you will feel the wind. There is a God and He is the Creator of all things (Isaiah 44:24). He is Sovereign and that means He is in control of this universe. Knowing those truths helps us all to settle into a peaceful rest in our souls. If God can build and sustain the universe He can sustain us. We are created by God in His image (Genesis 1:27). He arises up in our lives and shines His face on us. We can see God in His works and we can sense His touch. *Jesus said in John 14:27, "Peace I leave with you; My peace I give you. I do not give to you as the world gives. Do not let your hearts be troubled and do not be afraid."*

The peace that the world gives is momentary and fragile, it doesn't last. And that so called peace comes with thought processes of self design or whatever other way the world chooses to get it. But the peace of God is a GIFT given to those who receive it. God's peace is strong, lasting, and always present as God Himself is. So sit back, drink your coffee, breath a prayer, open the Bible, and let God show you His love and abilities to handle your life. Then, get up and do the day with God confidence and sing! I call this the beautiful life!

ª LINGERING in the LINES – Live in peace today

Jesus

JESUS – This name will always illicit a response. Some believe He is the Son of God coming to us in human form to connect us to our Heavenly Father. Some people believe Jesus is just another person in history along with Thomas Edison, Mother Teresa, Abraham Lincoln, and Leonardo da Vinci who made an impact on the world. Some people believe Jesus was a spiritual man and a prophet who was peddling a religion that was just one of many paths we could take in our search for spirituality. Some people are embarrassed at the mere mention of this name. Some people use this name in conversation that shows no regard, awe or reverence to the Name. That is how some people think and how some people act towards the name Jesus.

I would like to tell you what the name Jesus really means. One day at the mere mention of the Name every knee will bow and every tongue will confess that Jesus is Lord (Philippians 2:10). It is the Name that breaks the power of sin and death. It is the Name that comforts the sorrowing and restores the broken. It is the Name that calms the sea and woos the robin to sing. It is the Name that soothes the worried and releases the confused. It is the Name that blesses the children and rebukes the Pharisee. It is the Name that provides rest for the weary and satisfies the hungry. This is Almighty God the Creator of heaven and earth and everything in it (Isaiah 40:28). This is the Way, the Truth and the Life (John 14:6). There is no other name under heaven by which men shall be saved (Acts 4:12). And JESUS is His Name.

LINGERING in the LINES – Whisper the Name, Whisper the Name

Just Be

Sometimes we get tired. We have read the books, talked the talk, walked the journey, and prayed the prayers. When you get weary it will be the time when you will need to remember a few things. One of those things is to just be. We need a fresh realization that we are simply to be here at this time and place. God delights in His children and is just so happy that we are His. Our presence of just being is the joy. It is not all the doing and working and moving around that brings us contentment. It is just being.

This is the way it is with our walk with God. It is all about just letting God be present. Why not just sit back at this moment and enjoy God. We do not always need to see Him move and work and do for us to really get the relationship with God meaningful. We just need to let God be the presence of God in our lives. Enjoy His presence. Sit in His presence. Walk in His presence. Talk in His presence. Move in His presence. Live in His presence. Just let God be. He loves that kind of rich connection.

It is so refreshing to have someone seek you out not for what you can do but for just being you. God feels the same way. Just seek Him out to talk and shoot the breeze together. I like this kind of freedom in our relationship with God. It is that simple and it is that real! Try it!

LINGERING in the LINES – Be still and know today

Keep Christ

"*Today in the town of David a Saviour has been born to you; He is Christ the Lord.*" I hope this truth quoted from Luke 2 in the Bible is not overlooked by its overuse at this time of the year. We often hear about keeping the Christ in Christmas. I was pondering why is it so important that we keep the Christ in Christmas yet we leave the Christ out of our everyday life issues and lives. When we leave God out of our everyday lives what does the coming of Christ really mean? Does it mean that we as a culture are fine with Christ being in an unoccupied barn that is out of sight and out of mind? Does it mean that we as a culture are fine with Christ being the theme of a play to act in but not our personal experience? Does it mean we as a culture perform in concerts for the applause of people yet never seek the applause of God by singing the song of Christ?

When we leave Christ out of everyday issues we empty Christ of His rightful place in our hearts and minds. Many years ago a Saviour named Christ the Lord was born in the city of David. Today this Saviour can be born into each heart that receives Him as their Saviour. This is what it means to include God in the everyday issues of your life. Jesus has come to save us from our wrong attitudes, our pride, our wounded spirits, and our performance based insecurities. Jesus has come to be close to us and not in some out of sight and out of mind place far from our soul. Jesus has come close. This is the experience of Christmas. Let Christ shape your heart and not culture.

LINGERING in the LINES – Make Christmas a soul celebration

Keep the Perspective

What a strange thing it would be to clean up the locker room of a sports team and tuck away all the equipment in its proper place before the game began. How about the activity of putting all the prepared food for a party away in neat little plastic containers before the people arrived to eat it? Would you even consider this? You might if the clean up task was more important than what the people, the game and the party represent. We are to enjoy the people, the food and the decor of the party and we are to enjoy the game. We should enjoy the clean up too but only in its rightful order in our priorities. This is the life God has called us to.

Don't worry about the undone dishes but enjoy the great meal and the conversation around the table. Don't anticipate cleaning up the decorated room before you get a chance to enjoy all the creativity that went into it and the joy it brought to people. The moment of doing the next task will come but don't miss the moment you are in. It is more important to appreciate the people walking in and making your floor dirty than waiting to wash the floor. The floor getting dirty shows there is the activity of life and people in your world. The dirty dishes show that there is someone in your world to cook for. These are the moments to savour. Don't miss the point or you miss the life and the community of people!

LINGERING in the LINES – Live the moment

Waiting Womb-Waiting Room

There were women in the Bible who wanted to begin a family and for various reasons this desire and dream was not happening. These women did something as they waited. They prayed to God as they waited. They cried out to God as they waited. They questioned God as they waited. They worshipped God as they waited. They even doubted God as they waited. They all did something as they waited. We can use their examples for our own "waiting rooms" in life.

As these women were waiting, praying, crying out, worshipping, and doubting they received a reward. The reward was experiencing God as their only Source of help to do the impossible in their lives. The real reward is having a good and loving God to come to with everything that concerns us. When we make the living God first place in our lives everything else fits into its rightful order just like Jesus said it would (Matthew 6:33). Worries, fears, questions, and doubting are replaced with trust.

The work of waiting brought a few surprises as Hannah gave birth to the prophet Samuel who would lead God's people closer to God. Rachel gave birth to Joseph who would save God's people from starvation when a famine ravaged the land. Sarah gave birth to Isaac who would carry on the faith of his father. Bathsheba would give birth to Solomon who would lead God's people with more God given wisdom than any man who ever lived.

You may not have a "waiting womb" but I am sure you have some "waiting room" issue in your life.

LINGERING in the LINES – Do the work of seeking God in your waiting

Let Me Introduce You

In Luke 10:22 Jesus is telling us that He and His Father know each other in the family relationship of a father and a son. Jesus said that everything was committed to Him by His Father and that He would reveal His Father to people. Jesus wants to introduce His Father to you because He desires for you to be in the family of God. When we share family with God then His Holy Spirit can tell us things we cannot know on our own (Jeremiah 33:3).

When you read the Bible as words you get to know the facts. It is when we allow the words to be applied in a real personal experience we get the knowing or the essence of what God is saying to us. God shows Himself to those who want to see because they are the only ones looking. He cannot show Himself to a person who does not desire to see. The thing that causes us to desire to see is that we come to God as little children. If we try to come to God as people with a superior attitude we will not see God or know His deep and hidden treasures of truth.

Come to God small as a child coming to your Father in heaven. Let the Holy Spirit of Christ tell you who God is by making Him known to your soul. Come small and let a big God meet you there!

LINGERING in the LINES – Read Luke 10

Letter from a Friend

I began to read the letter from a friend and stopped to ponder each line written. One of the lines of the letter said, "I love you." Another line was, "Hope you can come soon, I am waiting to get together." Still another line read, "You are a friend to me and I have a wonderful surprise for you when you come." I was getting more and more excited as I read the letter.

I arranged my schedule and reunited with this true and trusted friend. It was like we had never been apart. We took up our conversation and camaraderie right where we had left it when we had been apart. One of us would tell everything that had been happening in our lives as the other listened. This went back and forth the whole time we were together. There is nothing like an old friend who is tried and true. As friends with shared experiences we could sit together drinking coffee and talking for hours. It is like being home. It is a bit of heaven.

May you arrange your schedule to meet with a true Friend (John 15:5). He is the One and only God who loves you and longs to meet with you (Deuteronomy 6:4).

God has written you a letter. Take time to ponder the lines. God has many surprises waiting for you. Grab a coffee on your way and enjoy sweet conversation as you pick up where you left off. Tell God everything that is happening in your life story. Then listen when He tells you His story. It is being home. It is heaven on earth.

LINGERING in the LINES – Make time for God

Life or Death

We can see death at the moment after birth. Cell death and renewal take place on a regular basis in our bodies. It is always a death and life situation. That is just what it meant when Eve would not listen to God and chose her own path to knowledge. Her deluded mind brought destruction to her and to the world. The beautiful garden called Eden was no longer her beauty. Eve along with her husband Adam had to leave the garden called home. As the couple left the garden the dying of everything began.

They soon had a son who chose death rather than life just like his parents had. He was named Cain and he purposefully chose to kill his brother Abel out of the death attitude of jealousy. God had previously warned Cain of the wrong attitude of his heart. God warned Cain to master this sin in his life. But Cain would not heed God's voice and he went ahead and acted on the sin in his heart. He killed his brother. When Cain chose this path it altered the good plans God had for his life. Now he would wander aimlessly about restless in soul simply because he refused to listen to God's correction (Genesis 4).

You and I no longer need to choose death to our souls. We cannot change that Eve caused death to happen to the world with her rebellion. What we can change is our choice to stay in that place of death or choose life. Jesus said that He came to bring life to us. Now because of Christ redeeming love we can choose God who is the Tree of Life (Genesis 3:22-24). God is merciful, kind, and good. He gave Eve another child to show His kindness to her. God gave Cain another chance too. God marked him so that no one would find Cain and kill him. God cared.

Were Adam, Eve, and Cain deserving of God's loving kindness? No, they were not and neither are we. The Bible says in Romans 3:23, *"For all have sinned and fallen short of the glory of God."* The Bible also says in I Corinthians 15:3, *"Christ died for our sins, He was buried and raised on the third day."* Here we are face to face with Christ dying to redeem our sin. Here we are face to face with the empty tomb of a resurrected Christ. Now we can be marked to live in the righteousness of Christ (Philippians 3:9). That is if we make the choice to do so.

God desires for each one of us to choose life (Deuteronomy 30:19). Will we do so is the question? The answer you and I give is a matter of life or death. Let us all purpose to choose Life and Jesus is His name. Bring back the beauty of Eden to your soul.

LINGERING in the LINES – Reorder your attitudes where need be

Losing Everything, Keeping Everything

In the last few years of my father's life he was losing everything. He was losing his hearing, he was losing his eyesight and he had lost the ability to do self care forcing the loss of his independence. He was losing everything that we consider so necessary in this life we live. Yet he was keeping everything! Paul said these words in Philippians 3:7, *"But whatever was to my profit I now consider loss for the sake of Christ. What is more, I consider everything a loss compared to the surpassing greatness of knowing Christ Jesus my Lord."*

My Dad knew his God and often expressed the joy of his desire to see his Heavenly Father face to face. That day did happen and that joy is his today. He has everything. When you make a personal relationship with God your everything, then you can see Him without physical eyes and you hear Him without physical ears. Even though you may not be able to take care of yourself physically, God is taking care of your eternal soul. God will provide the other care you need through the hands of people He places on earth.

Temporal things are going to get lost and change but the eternal God does not change or shift (James 1:17). He is not rendered powerless even when we are. In fact that is when He shines the most. When we lose the things of life we never lose the things of God! Take heart, because with God you keep everything that really matters!

LINGERING in the LINES –Thank God for His care and thank the people God is sending to help you

Loved by God

When you declare that Jesus loves you it will be a philosophy of life that will be the foundation for your journey to trust God despite how the issues of life go. Possibly you have read in the book of John in the Bible where John calls himself "the disciple who Jesus loved." At first glance you may have thought this to be arrogant attitude. I believe John had realized he was loved by God and this was his declaration of truth for his own life. This embraced truth would be the foundation of his life to trust God and it would forever shape his life and settle his soul. He was saying he was the disciple who Jesus loved because he was and so are you. You can say "_____ (put your name here) the disciple Jesus loves." This is a beautiful thing. *"For God so loved the world"* is for everyone and yet this statement here is very personal and individual.

May you allow this very personal love of God be your own declaration. Let God's love shape the remainder of your days. It is good to say you are the disciple Jesus loves because it is true. The next time you are faced with more criticism than love in your life look to the love of God and tell yourself the truth, "Jesus loves me this I know!"

LINGERING in the LINES – Tell someone that God loves them

Manger Cries

The gift of God sent to us was laid in a manger. He was laid in a manger which was a feeding trough for animals. How significant is this detail of Jesus birth. When He grew to adulthood He told the people of the world that they were to eat from Him. He alone declares Himself the Bread of Life. His cry from the manger bed is the food for our souls. The innkeepers were far too busy and preoccupied with many issues to make room for a baby and His cry. Make room for these cries from the heart of God.

"I will never leave you or forsake you."

"Come to Me all you who are weary and so burdened with care and I will give you rest."

"I love you and rejoice over you with singing and dancing."

"You are mine."

"I forgive you and cast all your sins into the deepest sea."

"Do not fear for I am with you."

"Do not be confused for I am your God."

"I have come that you may have life and life abundant."

"Be still and know that I am God."

May this Christmas be one where we see everything through the cries of Christ. In these cries we celebrate the coming of hope, healing, victory, peace, joy, mercy, love, and salvation.

LINGERING in the LINES – Do a verse search of these God declarations

Mother's Recipe

I found a recipe card the other day in my mother's handwriting. I was intrigued at the simplicity of the recipe. She had written part of the jam recipe ingredients as two margarine tubs of strawberries. That may seem strange since the size of container was not specified, but my mother knew the size. She had prepared this recipe before. In order for me to know I just had to ask. Possibly this kind of recipe writing has the flavour of the desire to connect and communicate. Possibly this kind of recipe writing was so that we could have a face to face relationship. My mother was the one knowing the answers about the recipe. I was the daughter needing to ask the questions so that she could share her knowledge with me.

When God wrote a recipe of how to do life called His Word He desired for each of us to connect with Him. He desires for us to communicate with Him and have a face to face relationship with Him. God wants us to ask Him how we are to apply His words to the various circumstances of our lives. He knows the recipe. Just ask God. Then enjoy the company of you and God together. Be sure to also enjoy the personal revelation that God wants to tell you (Jeremiah 33:3).

LINGERING in the LINES – Ask God for a personal word just for you

Mounted and Moved

When you see a cross what does it mean to you? If you walk through a multitude of graves marking those lost in many wars you will think of lives sacrificed for the cause of their country. There are other graves marked with a cross that indicates a personal loss of a loved one who left this earth. When you look at the cross mounted on a church your thoughts will turn to Christ. Even if people don't want their thoughts to do this they will. People will think this way because God is getting our attention with the cross.

Here at the cross we think of sacrifice for a cause and that cause was you. That cause was for your freedom from death and sin. Here at the cross we think of the death of our beloved one named Christ. The cross of Christ is the dividing line between what matters and what doesn't. The cross of Christ means death. It means death to human despair, guilt, loneliness and fear. Jesus was God in the skin of humanity and His coming to die conquered the sinful nature that holds back the spiritual nature from becoming alive and well. Jesus hung on the cross to separate our devotion from sin to God.

Jesus earthly death led to eternal life of an empty grave. Jesus said, "*I am the Resurrection and the Life.*" This is who He is. We will never have eternal life outside of Christ. God's desire for the world is to have this life and life abundant. All we have to do is say "yes" to the invitation. Christ in you is the hope of glory (Colossians 1:27). This is Good News indeed!

LINGERING in the LINES – Fix on Christ—His cross, His empty grave

New Year, New Adventures

The old year had many adventures. So why not keep this thing going. What is your goal for this New Year? Without a bit of direction you will miss the adventure. You will cease to hear the overtures of God and you will cease to see the activity of God all around you. So get away with God and talk to Him. Ask God a few things. Ask Him what His thoughts are towards you for the year you are entering. Ask Him what you should focus on. We don't have these answers if we do not ask. So ask (James 4:2). God wants to be seen and heard and it is our job to be open to that. Take the time to look and see, to watch and wait, and to listen and hear. This year I am walking into a year to see God fill my life with His good gifts of hope, joy, and peace. I am trusting God to do this.

I believe after a while we can get a bit empty. When that happens God needs to fill us with His good gifts from heaven. These good gifts are the real thing that keeps life real, satisfying, and eternal. This is my journey for this New Year and I hope it will be yours as well. The verse I am drawn to is found in Romans 15:13, *"May the God of hope fill you with all joy and peace as you trust in Him, so that you may overflow with hope by the power of the Holy Spirit."*

LINGERING in the LINES – Choose a Bible verse focus for this year

Present Tense

We go about life and do, do, do. We give of our resources and energy but we often don't take the time to sit in the presence of another and enjoy their company. What we all need is to talk to someone. We need to laugh with another, cry with another, share stories, offer helpful insight and sit in the company of another.

This is the truest picture of a real God as He longs to share the company of our active presence. God wants to talk to us. God desires to laugh with us. God wants to offer helpful advice and instruction to us. God desires to share the stories of His Word with us. God is there to weep with us when we cry. God just simply desires to sit in our company. He is that real and that personal.

Today, take the time and offer your presence to the God who longs for you. I invite you to take the time in the company of your God to allow His presence to wipe away your tears, carry your sorrows, and settle your fears. Take the time today to be in the company of your God and allow His presence to bring you joy and laughter.

Don't forget to offer your presence to all the people around you. They need your love, laughter, insight, and instruction. Keeping company with God will equip you to be in company with people. By the way, you too need the company of another as you allow them to share their love, laughter, insight, and instruction with you.

LINGERING in the LINES – Call someone to enjoy their company

Refreshingly Different

A man was blind and his sight restored with a mixture of spit and mud spread over his eyes. Jesus did that. He made a blind man see. The first time Jesus did it the man saw people like trees. Jesus spread His spit and His mud on the man's eyes again and this time he could see everything as it should be seen. It took more than one try. Jesus is showing us that when we need an area of our life healed it may take time. As you start to see progress in your unhealed issue don't give up but keep working at it (Mark 8:23-25).

A man was deaf and could hardly speak. Jesus took the man away from the onlookers and put His fingers in the man's ears and then spit and touched the man's tongue. Jesus looked to heaven with a deep sigh and said, "Be opened." Then, the man's ears were opened and his tongue was loosened to speak plainly. The finger of God is healing and the words of His mouth changes things (Mark 7:33-34).

The next time you have trouble hearing God speak to you and have trouble speaking to God open up His Word. As you open the pages of the Bible to seek God He will touch you with His words. The finger of God's Spirit will open your ears to hear and untie your tongue to speak. God does all of this because He wants a relationship with you. He wants to know you as a friend. Sometimes miracles are done in other names than the name of Christ. Jesus warned us not to get side tracked with those things. The miraculous thing is not so much that a deaf man hears or a blind man sees. The real miracle is that God reaches out and brings you home to Himself. The real miracle is God speaking to you and listening to you because you matter to Him.

LINGERING in the LINES – Follow Truth

Skin Deep

Sometimes when we are in a crisis or have an emotional issue we talk about needing someone with skin on to help us. This often means that just going to God with the issue is not enough. The help we want is from someone on earth and not an unseen Deity above us in a non-earthly atmosphere.

This is what makes Christmas such an exciting event in our world. "*In the beginning was the Word, and the Word was God. The Word became flesh and made His dwelling with us*" (John 1). As I read this Biblical narrative I see that God did come with skin on. Jesus came to earth in human skin.

"*Today in the town of David a Saviour has been born to you; He is Christ the Lord. And He will be called Wonderful Counsellor, Mighty God, Everlasting Father and Prince of Peace*" (Luke 2 & Isaiah 9).

This God with skin on felt all of our issues as He too lived on the earth He created. This God came to help us and to tell us what we need to know. In our confusions He is the Counsellor, in our restlessness He is the Prince of Peace and in our limited abilities He is the Mighty God.

The everlasting Father outlives every generation of mankind and so we can trust the Word that became flesh. We can trust God for everything we need on earth as it is in Heaven.

LINGERING in the LINES – Read Psalm 117

Something Bigger

There is an old hymn written by George A. Young. He and his wife were financially impoverished for quite some time. Finally it was made possible for him and his wife to build a house. Shortly after realizing this dream and moving into their home someone set fire to it and reduced it to ashes. The hymn is entitled, "God Leads Us Along."

We have floods and we have fires in our lives. We experience green pastures when life is sweet and we experience deserts when things turn sour. The greater thing is to be led along by God who is with us in the floods, fires, and deserts of life. In these sour places God gives us a sweet song. The sour place does not need to define us but the sweet song of knowing and trusting God should define us and it can. We don't all go through the same things in this life. We really do need something greater than what we see. The one thing we will all need is not a thing at all but a Person. The greatest Person who ever lived is the greatest story ever told! The old Sunday school rings true with its sweet song of "Jesus loves me this I know for the Bible tells me so." May you join me in declaring these words of amen and amen which means so be it, so be it!

LINGERING in the LINES – Find a quiet place and sing a hymn to God

Sore Muscles, Wrecked Knees, Sunburned & Tired

I just finished a week with our adult children coming home for a vacation. They played volleyball in an all-day tournament, another day of intense tennis matches, and the fence building in the yard. After these activities they spent the evenings groaning in pain from sore muscles, sunburned skin, wrecked knees, and fatigue. When it was all said and done they expressed their satisfaction in accomplishing what they had set out to do. They all said that the exhilaration of accomplishment was worth the pain.

So why should it be any different when God calls us to a task that needs to be accomplished. Don't shy away from the work of forgiving an offense. Don't shy away from the work of loving someone when you don't feel like it. Don't shy away from the work of being self controlled instead of indulging in destructive habits. Don't shy away from being kind instead of harsh in your words. Remember never to shy away from the work of being holy and pure in heart.

As you press on to accomplish what you set out to do you may get a bit burned from the actions of others. You may get a bit wrecked by their indifference towards you and you may get a bit sore from all the tension the work requires. But at the end of the day all the pain will have been worth it. It will be exhilarating because you accomplished what you set out to do which is to live your life according to God's design. God will be true to you. He will heal your aching soul and restless mind with His love and care. God will relieve the tension of the work with His peace.

LINGERING in the LINES -- Do the work

The Egg

The other day as I was working in our bookstore/café a lady ordered an egg wrap on a white tortilla shell. I proceeded to prepare the food and handed it to her. It was only later that I realized I had made her an egg sandwich on brown bread. I had heard her request but I was not focused enough to accomplish it as ordered. As I pondered this experience I realized how often we are like this to God. God gives us an instruction and we hear it but we are not focused enough on Him to carry it out as God says.

The Bible says that we are "to be still and know God" in order to be focused enough to hear the words of God. We will need to "be still and know" in order to carry out the words of instruction as God says to. "Be still and know" will never be replaced if we are to come near to God and God is to come near to us (James 4:8).

LINGERING in the LINES – Read Psalm 46

The Feast

Most of us I would assume love to eat. Food is a gift and our bodies need food. With as many varied palates as there are people we will experience foods that taste wonderful. There will be other foods that we would rather stay away from. We are as diverse as our foods. The chef is also a key factor in food taste and beauty. We are provided with restaurant guides that describe eateries and the foods they present. These guides will encourage us to dine or not to dine depending on our view of the foods listed on their menus. Each one of us will decide if we will act on their recommendations and views about their eatery.

I see this so much like God and His Word the Bible. God's truth is the food we need to eat. God prepares the table before us. He takes ingredients of peace, hope, love, faith, sorrows, joys, and wisdom and puts them together as a feast for our souls. This is a feast of strength, perseverance, patience, and power. God places all of this good food before us and He invites us to dine.

People's views about the Bible and God will make God tasty to us or not depending on how we view the menu of truth. We may not like the food item on the menu that tells us to forgive the wrongs done against us. We may not like the food item on the menu that tells us to love God more than anything else on the whole earth. We may not like the food item that tells us not to lie. We may not like the food item that asks us to be available to help another person when we may have other plans.

The place we want to eat at and the food we desire to eat is entirely up to each one of us. But possibly you have not been completely informed about this God eatery of truth. Possibly you do not know or have not heard that eating at the eatery of God is a no cost event with an all you can eat buffet. The buffet is overflowing with the food of life and life abundant.

Possibly you do not know or have not heard that this eatery is rated with so many stars that they cannot be counted. You will never get a bad meal at the table of God because God's food never spoils. There are places that you will get sick at if you eat there. These places are the eateries of a self designed life and any place where truth is not served. Our Master Chef is named Truth. He knows the way to the best food because He is called the Way.

I have gone to this eatery of God and I find the menu tantalizing and mouth watering. I have eaten. I am satisfied. In fact my cup overflows. I give you my recommendation but the decision to go to this feast is up to you.

LINGERING in the LINES – Fill your soul with God's food today

The Elements

The table is set. The juice is poured. The bread is baked. It is a remembrance. We walk up to the communion table to take and eat, to take and drink. And then we remember. We remember that we have a grudge towards our friend. We remember that we were harsh in how we talked to our child. We remember that we were disrespectful to our boss or spouse. We remember how we criticized the pastor. We remember how our eyes rolled at the fellow with no job. We remember our anger over a misunderstanding. We remember our superior attitude towards someone over a mistake they had made but we had not made. We remember.

We reach for the table and take the juice and the bread and hold it cautiously with a trembling hand. What are we to do with the remembrance of our unholy behaviour? We are to remember Christ crucified and the power of His resurrection. In the dying of Christ for our unholy sins we obtain His holiness and we remember. In the resurrection of Christ from the grave we walk away from the death of our failings and sins and receive new life. We remember. As we remember the Christ of this table before us we repent and make declarations to our Saviour. I will with God's help cease from creating the ugliness of judgment on another, harsh words, angry outbursts, rolling eyes, disrespect and criticism to one such as I. I repent and I declare. This is the remembrance that Jesus seeks from each one of us.

LINGERING in the LINES – Say the words I repent and I declare

The Greats

So often when we are talking about great people we will mention the people of history who won wars, fed the starving, secured a cure for disease, or reinvented the wheel in some way. These are notable people and their contributions are applauded and should be. I know many people who have changed my world. I applaud them for their notable contributions. I consider them "The Greats."

I have had pastors, mentors, friends and family that have made my world a better place. I had a pastor who saw me one Wednesday evening sitting in church waiting for the service to begin. This pastor came up to me and asked if he could get me a cup of coffee while I was waiting. He saw me and served me. I still remember it. His pastoral care and concern for his flock is a moment I recall with clarity. He changed my world that evening. The pastor cared. The pastor served. I saw Jesus in action.

I had a mentor when I was a young wife and mother. She walked me through many issues of life. She encouraged me bringing out the best in me as she helped me work on the worst in me. She changed my world. She persevered in her commitment to care. I saw Jesus in action.

I have friends and family who are to be applauded for their notable contribution of sharing their lives with me. I know their names. They have changed my world. I urge you to share your life with another and as you do may the people see Jesus in action.

LINGERING in the LINES – Read 1 Thessalonians

The Job Journal - Anchored by Faith

Job was a suffering man from the Bible. This is what Job says of God, *"Even now my witness is in heaven; my advocate is on high. My intercessor is my friend as my eyes pour out tears to God. Though he may slay me, yet will I hope in Him. Indeed, this will turn out for my deliverance. I will wait for renewal to come."*

Even among all the questions of why and what have I done to deserve this Job knew where his help would come from. Despite all of his questions and confusions over the situations of his life he was confident in the truth. He knew that God would be his ultimate help and would breakthrough at some point. God did just that. He broke through and conquered the enemy attack with giving Job the heart to keep the faith.

The evil one hates it when we have faith in God and His truth. My mother used to say that if we resist Satan long enough he gets tired of us and walks away. When we resist the evil one God steps in to honour our obedience to His truth. God applauds us for our love to Him (James 4:7). God comes to us and calls us friend and says, "Well done, good and faithful servant." It is then that we see restoration and renewal happen from our unseen faith. Look for it and wait for it! Keep the faith and love the Lord!

LINGERING in the LINES – Read Hebrews 6

The Job Journal
- The Attack

In the Bible there was a man named Job. This fellow had spent his life knowing God. Job saw God's greatness and knew he needed God. They had grown tight with one another in a heart to heart relationship. As the story unfolds we see how important knowing God's character really is to our lives. One day something difficult will come into your life and then you will see if you believe who God is. We believe God by trusting in His character as the Bible tells us who God is.

Job was enjoying a beach day when out of the blue an evil attack happened on his possessions, powerful influence, and on his personhood. This attack was not because of wrong he had done but because Job was a child of God. We have a loving God in Heaven who loves the world and when the children of God suffer so does the Father of the children. God in Heaven had to watch the attack because evil was attacking God too.

I believe God was holding the armrests of His Throne praying for Job that he would not forget the character of his God. God was hoping that Job would not forget how much God really loved him. God grips His Throne knowing He is above all things. God waits in expectation for us to remember His love and not mess up God's character with our views about tragedy. Job came through this attack and conquered evil with his faith and did not charge God with wrong doing. Yeah Job! And when you follow this example of a strong real Biblical person then you too with get the high five, thumbs up yeah!

LINGERING in the LINES – Know God and conquer issues with faith

The Job Journal
- The Friends

In the book of Job, in the Bible we see a righteous man suffering from many life losses. At one point he is suffering so much physically that he is scraping his body with pieces of pottery in an attempt to diminish the intense pain. The Bible says that several friends were sitting with him. What were the friends doing? Well, at first they were quiet and sat beside Job to share in his suffering. But then there was a shift in their allegiance and they bombarded Job with judgmental questions and harsh advice. What these friends didn't do was help a suffering man by rubbing his wounds and giving Job the ability to rest. What these friends didn't do was comfort Job with kindness, grace, gentleness, and understanding.

When I was suffering from being burned in a fire, my mother spent the nights rubbing my burns which allowed me to have rest. This was what I needed. I did not need my mom to tell me how difficult life was and why this was happening. My mother used her hands to be the hands of Christ in my pain. This is what Job needed as well. What our suffering friends need from us is loving support with no judgmental attitudes or platitudes.

Sometimes we need to be the hands of healing in a situation. Sometimes we need to just feel the pain of others with our heart. Sometimes we need to help people think through their issues and we use our minds in that situation. I call this our mission of the Head, the Heart and the Hands. This is the mission of Christ and it is always wrapped in love.

LINGERING in the LINES – Help someone today in word, deed or both

The Owner
Based on Mark 12:13-17

There were a group of people who were trying to trap the God who created them. They were people who thought their ways, ideas, and views were better than God's. They were proud people on a mission to trip up God. They said, "Teacher, we know that You are a man of integrity. You aren't swayed by men, because You pay no attention to who they are but should we pay taxes to Caesar or not?"

Jesus tells these men to give Him a coin. Then Jesus asks them to tell Him whose inscription is on the coin. They tell Him it is Caesar's. Jesus tells them to give to Caesar what is his and to give to God what is God's. Here Jesus is telling them that people belong to God. God values people. This group of people were wrong when they told Jesus that He paid no attention to people. God cares. God pays attention. God knew each person long before they were born. God knows you.

You were made for God so give God all of you. Give God your views, your attitudes, your plans, your relationships, your future, and your questions and watch God make your life work.

These fellows spoke truth when they said that God is not swayed by men and their views. God's ways and thoughts are higher than our thoughts and ways and far above our reasoning (Isaiah 55:8-9). God never has been and never will be trapped by human opinions or hidden agendas. This is the confidence you can have in trusting God with your life.

LINGERING in the LINES – Be open with God about everything

The Purpose

We are in a pursuit of purpose. In your encounters with people you will hear people talk about their purpose and why they are here on this planet. Many times people will go after a cause to find their purpose. Some will go from job to job trying to find that niche that will give them purpose. When this is our view of purpose we will search endlessly for the "it" and that "it" will never reach its potential in being our purpose. Purpose is not a doing or a thing but a knowing and a loving. It is getting to know the God who created you and loving the Person that He is.

When we make the knowing and loving of God our pursuit we will have the purpose we all long for. From that high purpose God will move you into activities that He has personally arranged for you to do (Ephesians 2:10). Your primary purpose is to know and love God as the priority of your life. Then the things you do are simply the fruitful outcome of the greater thing of a relationship with God.

LINGERING in the LINES – List God's character traits as the Bible shows

The Song of_____
(Based on Song of Songs)

Fill in the blank. In the Bible there is a book called the Song of Songs penned by the wise King Solomon. That book is a love story using earthly language to convey spiritual truths about God and His love. Whenever you decide to ponder the love of God call your ponderings "The Song of _____" and put your name in the blank. I agree with Solomon's view that love causes the heart to skip a beat and the eyes to gaze upon the loved one and the words to pour forth in praise and admiration of the loved one. This is how "The Song of Laura" feels about God.

As a young child I saw God come to me and dignify me with His desire for my life to be involved with His own life. It was then that my heart skipped a beat. Can someone really love me this much? God's answer is yes! God loves us with such depth that His gaze is ever upon us. His love is so strong that He aches with emotion. This kind of love actually hurts. The cross of Christ shows us that hurt. This is a good hurt. This is a redeeming hurt. This is love! This love of God is not based on how well we act today. As we experience this love we will be moved to please this Lover with all that we do and say. God climbed down from the palm tree of heaven to get hold of us and secure our love. Now we can climb up the Tree of Christ and take hold of the God who loves us!

LINGERING in the LINES – Read the Song of Songs in the Bible

Awake

I went on an evening walk a few days ago and on that walk I started to think about God and how He thinks according to His words to us. In Psalm 121 the Bible says that the Lord watches over our lives and does not sleep or slumber. Since God is so passionate to watch over us would it not be appropriate to watch for God? He does not sleep concerning us and our issues of life. Maybe just maybe we shouldn't sleep over God's issues and His life. God has something to say to each one of us. Would it not be considerate of us to listen to God?

Do we regard God and His moral laws enough to work those laws into each of our lives? At any point of sin there is an infinite God with forgiveness, restoration, hope, and love showing up all over the place in our lives. At any point that we regard God's ways and receive His words we are awake. We are awake to an infinite and loving God who is calling out from the very place of Heaven itself and saying, "Well done!" This affirmation of love is heard in the very heart of the soul. Are you awake? God is!

LINGERING in the LINES – Sit by a lake and ponder the Creator

Soup or Sandwich

When we go to a restaurant it usually indicates we are hungry. When we arrive we need to go into the place in order to eat. We would never think of standing outside the door expecting that we will be served. We need to go in. This is no different than the journey of prayer to God. We will need to enter into prayer to make our requests.

After entering the restaurant you will need to place your food order to satisfy your hunger. You may order a ham sandwich only to receive a bowl of soup. You probably will inform the server that this is not what you ordered. Sometimes we ask God for things but we get something totally different then what we asked for. This reality can cause many people to leave prayer behind. The issue here is not if you get a bowl of soup or a sandwich but if your hunger is satisfied. As long as hunger is satisfied your need has been met. This is the confidence in prayer. God will meet your needs but they may not be met exactly the way you requested (Romans 8:26-27; Philippians 4:19).

In the end the thing that matters is that your needs have been met and your hunger satisfied. How this is accomplished is not what matters. God knows best how to meet our needs. By faith we can trust the words from a very good and kind God. In Matthew 7:7 it says, *"Ask and it will be given you, for everyone who asks receives."*

So make a decision to never give up on prayer to God. God will provide what you need the way you need it according to His will and perfect knowledge. It will not matter if it is a bowl of soup or a sandwich because you will be fed. You will be satisfied and your need will be met.

LINGERING in the LINES - Memorize Matthew 7:7 & 8

Worse Sin

There is always a question in the minds of people of what is the worst sin we could commit. Sometimes in our Pharisee ways we decide which sins are the worst to judge. Jesus always has the answers to our questions. Jesus had a close friend named Judas who betrayed Him to the authorities. Judas betrayal caused Jesus to be arrested. Jesus was then brought before a man named Pilate. Pilate was the one to decide if the charges against Jesus were worthy of His death. Pilate found nothing to warrant death but the religious leaders were pushing for it. The religious leaders had influence and so Pilate caved into their demands. These were the sins of the people to a holy God.

Yet Jesus told Pilate that Judas was guilty of a greater sin (John 19:10-11). The greater sin is the sin of the heart. Judas had a betraying heart to God and did not regard Christ. Pilate had committed a sin of the human nature called people pleasing. The greatest sin we can do is to turn our backs on God with a decision to do so. That is the greatest sin because it takes away your destiny of life eternal. David was called a man after God's own heart even though he had had an adulterous affair with another man's wife. The affair was a sin of his flesh or of his earthly nature. David never denied God. He knew God was the answer to his soul. He always knew that. All sin hurts both God and you but the greater sin is the sin of the betraying heart.

LINGERING in the LINES – Do you love God with all of your heart?

Welcome Home

We are moving rapidly to the end of this year and to the beginning of another. Before we close this year we are going through the Christmas season. What can we do to prepare for a meaningful Christmas? When we get ready for the birth of a child in our home we prepare a room. This room has a crib and other things needed to give this baby a beautiful life of belonging in our home.

It should be no different with the expectant arrival of God coming to us as a baby born on earth. God needs to be welcomed into the home of your soul. When you do that God can have a beautiful life on earth as He has in heaven. What are you doing in your attitudes and actions that will give God a beautiful home in you?

Are you forgiving the person that has hurt and wronged you? Are you loving the difficult person in your life? Are you waking up each day in wonder at the creation around you? Are you thankful in everything? Are you kind? Are you in awe of God's character? Are you smitten with God's love given to you? Are you excited to read God's words to you in the Bible? Are you faithful to the commitments you make? Are you peaceful?

The answers to these questions will let you know if you are consistently preparing a beautiful room for God to live in or not. God is the master of beautiful. When we follow God's directives and live by them we will develop a beautiful life.

LINGERING in the LINES – Rearrange your attitudes to answer YES to the above questions.

What Will People Say

What will people say about you when you have left this space called earth? Will they say that you placed people ahead of yourself looking towards their interests more than you own? Will they say that you loved the people around you despite their personality quirks? Will they say you were generous with all the resources God had given you? Will they say you treated them with kindness? Will they say you were tender and gentle of heart?

God says that He looks on the heart and not on the outward appearance of things (I Samuel 16:7). This means that we need to work on the attitudes of our heart. We should all purpose to leave a legacy behind that has walked in the footsteps of Jesus with a heart like Jesus. We may come to the realization that we are not leaving a legacy like this but there is always a way to change that. Jesus came to create in us a new heart (Psalm 51:10). He is the power we need to change. If we are stingy we can begin to give and be generous with our resources. If we are negative or ill tempered we can begin to be positive and calm in our responses. If we are unforgiving we can begin to forgive offenses done to us.

God is with us in word and presence showing us how to change. Our attitude should be that of Christ who humbled Himself by becoming a servant who fed the hungry and blessed the broken (Mark 8). Our attitude should be that of Christ who is gentle and humble in heart. Our attitude should be that of Christ who turned the tables of disregard and injustice upside down (Matthew 21:12). Make a decision to leave a legacy of the heart.

LINGERING in the LINES – Fix your eyes on Jesus

Why Pray?

We are called to pray because God said we should. Prayer is needed if we want to know God and find help to overcome the difficult issues of life. We need prayer in order to receive the gifts of joy, hope, peace, significance, and everlasting life that God desires to give to each one of us.

When we rely on the world to give us what only heaven can give we are sorely disappointed. The world cannot give us the things that come from the loving heart of God. Jesus said these words, *"Peace I leave with you; My peace I give you. I do not give as the world gives"* (John 14:27). The world or culture will tell you things that you will need to do or buy to get its version of peace and happiness. Jesus tells us that He is the true peace for the soul of a person. We cannot buy it but we can ask God for it and receive it.

You may wonder from time to time why God would make you ask Him for things you need (Matthew 7:7). God is not a cruel God of withholding but how can He give something you do not seek after. You may want to give me a table but I do not want it. The gift will be wasted on me and will sit in a hidden storage room gathering dust. God does not waste any of the things He gives. Remember how the disciples gathered all the leftovers from a large feast that Jesus was responsible for. Jesus expressed to the disciples to waste nothing (John 6:12). God is not going to waste His gift of peace on those who do not seek it. If He did that peace would lay gathering dust as your choice of worry and frustration would rule your situation.

LINGERING in the LINES – Ask for heavenly gifts to come to your soul

Born Identity

You are known. You have an identity and it goes beyond what people see. It goes deeper than the surface and it is known only to God. This God who knows you identifies you. He calls you by name and tells you that you are dearly loved (Isaiah 43).

The Bible says God formed us and knew everything about us before one of our days came into existence (Psalm 139). God tells us who we are and He never gets it wrong. We can trust the God who knows all things. He tells it like it really is. This is a beautiful thing.

Sometimes we may not believe the beauty of it when we are doing things that we want to hide. Things like saying smooth words with the mouth but having war in our hearts (Psalm 55:21). Our inability to hide from God's knowledge allows God to redirect what we are doing or thinking towards His better, right, and good way. God and His ways is the beauty, always the beauty.

The garden shows its beauty when the weeds are pulled and the water flows freely over the planted things. The house shows its beauty when the windows are clean and the dust is removed. The dinner shows its beauty when the food is prepared and cooked with flavourful herbs and spices. The relationships of your life will show the beauty when you are real in faithfulness, in forgiveness, in loving, in being kind, and all the desires that God identifies with. Let the beauty of living as God says to live be the cry of your heart. Please do not hide from this beauty! This is your identity. You were born for this.

LINGERING in the LINES – Read Psalm 19

The Faithful Few

"Help is on the way" is a motto I carry for a friend. She has the gift of helps and the other day it showed. She was driving past my parked car at my work and noticed that the tire was flat. She stopped and came to tell me of my problem. Not only did she inform me of my problem she had the solution to help me. She had a portable machine that would put air in my tire and then I would be able to get home after work. We attached the machine to the car for power and with her knowledge the problem was attended to and helped.

This is the story of God. He saw that we had a problem that wouldn't allow us to get home to His house. He stopped by the earth to inform us we had a problem. Not only did He inform us but He had the solution to help us. He attached Himself to the cross with the power of His love that secured our forgiveness and eternal life.

One day we will leave the work of earth and God will bring us home to that eternal dwelling place. God noticed we had a problem. God stopped to tell us. God had the knowledge of how to get us out of our problem and attended to us with His love, help, care, and concern. Can we do any less for the God who created us and calls us by name? (Isaiah 43:1)

LINGERING in the LINES – Notice a need and help

A Treasure of Trust

In the Bible when God's people were travelling through the desert there was no food. God provided sweet wafer like bread from heaven itself. The people were to gather enough bread for the day but no more. When people were not satisfied with the daily provision they gathered double. Possibly they did this because of fear that it would not come again tomorrow. Or they may have just been greedy to get more than was necessary. Whatever the reason may be their strategy did not work. When they gathered more than their daily need their food became full of maggots and proved worthless (Exodus 16).

The issue of this story is not so much about provision of bread for hunger but about trusting God enough to obey His words. When God speaks to us they are valuable words that require our attention. God speaking to us is a rich treasure of provision for our souls. When we do not listen to God's instructions His very good words prove to be worthless to us. God's words are a treasure but only to those who trust and obey. Why did these people not trust the God who created the bread?

God wants a daily walk of obedience from us. Our obedience to God is the provision. Jesus who is called the "Bread of Life" taught us how to pray to our Father who is in heaven, "*Give us this day our daily bread*" (Matthew 6:11). I urge you to obey what God is telling you. God knows what you need. Your obedience to what God knows will meet your needs.

LINGERING in the LINES – Read Matthew 7

Heart Check

When we think about living a purposeful life we often believe we need to accomplish great things or else what we do does not matter. We decide in our own minds and by the culture around us what great really is. I have friends whose careers were school teachers and nurses. All these women have completed work in their vocations and now love to serve coffee in our Bookstore / Café. The definition of great to them is not a position title but serving people with a coffee, a smile, and kindness.

There is no job too menial that does not have purpose. It all matters. Purpose is about the attitude that you do everything with. It's about the heart. Jesus the God of the Universe and the Lord of all said that He came to serve. Jesus did not think it too menial to prepare a lunch for over 5,000 people even though He was a Teacher of Biblical truth. Jesus did not think it too menial to wash the feet of His disciples even though He was King of kings.

God says that we should not seek great things for ourselves because when we do it keeps us from seeking the greater thing of living out the character of God in our lives (Jeremiah 45:5).

LINGERING in the LINES – Read Genesis 1

I Prayed

At my mother's funeral her brother was telling us a few stories about my mother. He mentioned that my mother had prayed for him to become a Christian. It took a bit of time but my uncle did come to faith in Christ. My uncle asked my mother what gave her the confidence to believe that one day she would see him become a new creation in Christ (2 Corinthians 5:17). My mother responded with these words, "I prayed."

That is our confidence too. When you pray in God's will and for God's will you too can say "I prayed." This is a picture of faith. Faith believes what it asks for before it is seen. When it comes to praying for those who do not have a personal relationship with Christ we can be assured the prayer for that to happen is in God's will. The Bible says that God is not willing that any be lost for He has come to seek and save the lost. It also says, *"For God so loved the world that He sent His Son" (John 3:16).* The Bible tells us that Jesus the Son willingly came because Jesus loves people just as His Father does.

God loves people and wants everyone close to His heart. Let us pray for people to respond to God's love. God's love is there for everyone but people need to respond to the invitation of God with a "yes." When you pray for someone to say "yes" to God and they do, don't be too surprised. Just answer as my mother did, "I prayed."

LINGERING in the LINES – Read I John 5:14 & 15.

1, 2, 3 and Counting

Jesus is called "The Word" because words matter. They affect us. God spoke 4 words to a dark earth, "Let there be light" and there was. Our dark situation may be a negative attitude. When we welcome God's 4 words of "Let there be light" we get perspective on why we have this dark issue of negativity. God will impress on our hearts and enlighten us that ungratefulness is causing us to be negative. The light of God's Word will be our instruction to be joyful always and to give thanks in all circumstances (I Thessalonians 5:16-18). Then as we walk in the light with obedience to God there will be no more darkness of negativity in our lives.

There was a friend of Jesus named Peter. Peter was in a boat that was being tossed about by a fierce storm and he was afraid. He saw Jesus walking on water towards him and asked Jesus if he could join Him. Then Jesus spoke 1 word, "Come." Peter stepped out of the boat and walked on the water just like Christ. Peter saw Jesus as the powerful One and knew that he needed that power to conquer his fears. When you answer God's call to "Come" to Him with your storms of life fears you will be able to walk on the water with God. God says these 4 words to you, "Do not be afraid" (Matthew 14).

When you have failed in some way why not look up to heaven and say 7 words to God, "Lord, have mercy on me a sinner." As you read the truth of God's words in the Bible look up to heaven and say 2 words, "I believe." Words matter, yours and God's!

LINGERING in the LINES – Speak to the God of Heaven today

Just Right

There is so much to do and sometimes we may get overwhelmed with it all. God has a remedy for us and it is in Deuteronomy 33:25 where it says that our strength will equal our days. I have experienced so many times having a large, difficult and intense task to do and God gave large strength to accomplish it. When my tasks were not so large I was given small strength for that was all that was necessary. The need is what God looks at and then in wisdom God supplies everything to meet that need. God does it just right!

When I was training for a ten kilometre run I had two goals. One goal was to do short runs to build up speed. The other goal was to do long runs to build up endurance. On the day of my short runs I just made it through but I made it. Then on the day of the long run I wondered how I would do it because the short run had been so hard. But God supplied and I just kept on running farther and farther each time. I needed more strength for the long run and I received it.

God supplies strength as our days and activities need it. We have no need to worry but only trust. God proves Himself to be true because He cannot lie. This is Someone you can trust 100% of the time.

LINGERING in the LINES – Read John 6

My Dad

When my father was 91 years old he was weak and resting in his bed. I had just returned from a short holiday weekend and went over to my parent's home to see them. As I walked into the room to greet my Dad he started to weep. He kept telling me over and over again how glad he was to see me. His very words were "I am so glad to see your face again." Truly there is something so very special and powerful about love and affirmation. It gives us a sense of belonging and purpose. It builds a healthy self-esteem making the world a beautiful place.

The way my father reacted to me is the way our Heavenly Father reacts to us. God longs to have His children come to His side and to greet Him with a life of devotion and conversation. When we talk to God in prayer about everything God tells us a similar thing like my earthly father said to me. God says in Song of Songs 2:14, *"Show me your face, let me hear your voice; for your voice is sweet and your face is lovely."*

Who can resist a Father like this? The love and affirmation of God towards you makes your world a beautiful place. So purpose to look up into the face of the Father of your soul and allow Him the joy of seeing your face.

LINGERING in the LINES – Read Zephaniah 3:17

The Fit

There may be times when you go to church and you feel like you do not belong. Possibly you have no position or anything you feel can contribute to the overall workings of the church. Sometimes we get discouraged because we feel lost in the pew. Sometimes we feel we are not needed because we are not on a committee. Sometimes we sit in church desiring to use the gifts and abilities God has given us but there is no opportunity to use them. When this happens to us we disengage our minds and hearts from this thing called the church. When we disengage apathy soon enters our personality and the next step may be to quit going to church at all. Or at the very least we may keep going to church yet feel completely alone and useless.

If this is how you feel I want to encourage you. You matter. God made you to matter. He alone rules our worth. Just you sitting on that church chair or pew will make you a part of this thing called the church. Just you walking through the doors of the church will make you a part of this thing called the church. Just your voice singing with the worship team will make you a part of this thing called the church. Just you listening with a hearing ear to the preacher will make you a part of this thing called the church. Just you shaking the hand of an usher that greets you will make you a part of this thing. Your presence at church matters to God regardless of how you may think. God's view is the final say on this thing. Please don't ever forget that. You matter. You matter. Take that truth and renew your mind with it the next time you feel like you don't fit. Just being in church says you fit!

LINGERING in the LINES – Read Psalm 139

Up and Around

Song of Songs 2:6 says, "*His left arm is under my head, and his right arm embraces me.*" This verse shows us the character of God in His desire to care, connect, and protect. This is your God. He places His left hand under your head and lifts your head from the thoughts of self and the world. He lifts your head so that you can think out of the mind of Christ that has been given to you (1 Corinthians 2:16). His left hand holding up your head is God bringing His truth to your mind so that you can live by that truth. This is His up protection given to you from His hand alone.

God's right arm embraces you with His all around love showing you His care and connection. God the King of kings embraces you with His right hand showing you that you have royal identity. You are a royal priesthood (1 Peter 2:9). God desires us to live with uplifted heads filled with humble confidence in our God given position of royalty.

LINGERING in the LINES – Read Daniel 6

What Good Is A Title?

What if you had the title "teacher" but never taught, the title "nurse" but never helped the sick, the title "carpenter" but never built, the title "secretary" but never handled the details of an office or the title "cook" but never prepared a meal? The title means nothing unless you do what the title indicates. The same holds true for the title "Christian." What does it mean when we own this title Christian and yet hold grudges instead of forgiving offenses, demeaning people instead of encouraging them, hating someone instead of loving them, or judging people instead of showing understanding?

The world is helped and good is accomplished when teachers teach, nurses care, carpenters build, secretaries organize, and cooks prepare meals. The world is changed and God is loved when Christians live as the title indicates—like Christ. And really, in the end, the title is only as good as the activity that results from what you say you are.

LINGERING in the LINES – Read 2 Timothy 1

The Gravity of Truth

What brings security to you? Is it certain people, or personal doings or your own view of things? On this earth there is a law called gravity. Gravity keeps earthly things secured into position so we have order and stability. Here we see an invisible law having a visible effect. Our furniture stays visibly grounded from flying all over the place because of the gravity we do not see.

The invisible God secures His position of unseen truth and it has a visible effect all around us. God keeps us ordered in the gravity of His truth so that we don't fly off in a thousand different directions in confusion at all the religious, cultural, and personal views out there.

The Bible says, "*Therefore we do not lose heart though outwardly we are wasting away, yet inwardly we are being renewed day by day. So we fix our eyes not on what is seen, but on what is unseen*" (2 Corinthians 4:17). So what are the unseen things of God that keep us grounded in the soul?

The unseen things are attitudes of heart and mind that changes a person's outlook even though the circumstance may still remain. God promises to turn mourning into gladness, pain into purpose, chaos into peace, despair into hope, wounds into healing, and hate into love. Peter told Jesus that He was the One with the words of truth and life. Peter also told Jesus that there was nowhere else to go to. We need to say this to God too, "There is nowhere else to go" (John 6:68).

LINGERING in the LINES – Read Psalm 84

Follow Love

Everyone has an issue or two in their attitudes of the heart. What is yours? Is it jealousy, competition with someone, comparing yourself to someone else, distain, anger, or discontent over your life? You name it because only you know what you are dealing with. The answers for all of these issues are in the Book of God. The words of God are life to us and they have the answers to heal all of our bad attitudes.

How can these words of God change our attitudes? God's words work because God knows how the human heart works and what it needs. There was a man named Peter in the Bible who had a jealous attitude. Peter felt like he was less than when he was around a certain man named John. Peter was troubled with his attitude and asked Jesus what he should do about it.

Jesus replied, "Peter, do you love Me?" Peter answered "yes." Then Jesus said to Peter, "Follow Me." Your love towards God will win over other loves especially the love of cherishing sin in your heart. God shows no favouritism. He thought up each individual person long before the foundation of the earth was created. This truth that "Jesus loves me this I know" stirs my heart to love God back. Peter answered "yes" to loving Christ and now he would be able to follow Jesus. Peter would now be able to follow Jesus without competition and jealousy towards another fellow follower. Peter knew he mattered to God and that would be enough (John 21:15-19).

When you say "no" to any thoughts or actions that are not consistent with the walk of Jesus Himself you win joy and victory!

LINGERING in the LINES – Read John 21

Impressions of God

As I read God's Book the words leave an impression on me. When I read in *John 15* about Jesus being the Vine and His people the branches, it is impressed upon my soul that we are connected and never alone.

When I read in *Job 39* about what God does in causing the horse to leap like a locust and the eagle to soar and build his nest on a high cliff at God's command, it is impressed upon my soul that God creates.

When I read in *Matthew 8* about a man with an incurable disease and a man paralyzed all made well, it is impressed on my soul that God truly can heal and do all things.

When I read in *Hebrews 11* that people with faith in God and His abilities did not see what they were hoping for accomplished, it is impressed upon my soul that God waits too for unseen to be seen.

When I read in *Hebrews 11* that prostitutes, murderers and weak people were all changed into new people with a new identity as faith filled children of God, it is impressed upon my soul that God includes everyone and welcomes us all to His heart.

When I read in *Revelation 21* that a new world will be accomplished by God's power with no more death or pain for the old order of things will be over, it is impressed on my soul that God wins because He is above all things.

LINGERING in the LINES – Let these truths settle into your soul

A Lost God

I am smitten with the season and reason for Christmas. So it should be no surprise to you that I will use a wee Christmas story in July. We have all heard of the slogan Christmas in July and as I write this I will embrace that slogan.

Many years ago God visited us from heaven with His earthly birth named Jesus. One day his earthly parents went to a festival with their extended family. The gathering was very large and in the busyness of that event the parents assumed that Jesus was traveling in the company of another family member. When Mary the mother of Jesus went looking for her son she could not find Him in the company of other family members. He was lost. They returned to the town they had been at. There they found Jesus sitting in the place where the truth of God's Word was being spoken and taught. God never has been lost. He is right where He belongs in loving the truth. Jesus is the Truth. That is His name and that is who He is. We will be the lost ones when we look anywhere but to the Truth for our help. As soon as we go to God we find everything we need for every issue in our lives. Jesus said that He came to seek and save the lost (Luke 19:10).

LINGERING in the LINES – Name a problem, speak a prayer, trust a promise of God

The Drought

Do you feel spiritually dry? If you answer yes to this question let me encourage you with the truth of God's Word. When we say we are "dry" we may be listening to the lies that can come from our emotions. In the last several weeks of my mother's life she was unable to drink or eat. I was watching this extreme demise as her body endured no water or food. It was at one of these bedside vigils that God impressed on me the truth of what was happening to my mother. The verse that God brought to my heart and mind was in *Isaiah 58:11, "The Lord will guide you always; He will satisfy your needs in a sun-scorched land and will strengthen your frame. You will be like a well-watered garden, like a spring whose waters never fail."*

God was telling me that my mother was being well-watered in her soul by God who was in her and with her. There was more going on then what I was seeing before my eyes. God is above and beyond the earthly issues of our lives. I leaned in close to my mother and whispered this verse over and over again into her ear. I was telling mother that I knew God was watering her soul in this earthly desert of dying.

God has vowed to commit Himself to our souls. God will never be unfaithful to His vows to love, honour, and cherish His children until death does us part from this earthly realm. I trust that you will never listen to the lie that you are "dry." You may be in a desert earth but you are never dry in soul, never! Jesus who is the Living Water is in you and His life is flowing freely to water your soul (John 4:10-13).

LINGERING in the LINES – Believe Truth until death parts you from earth

Always a Winner

As I write this I have just finished participating in a ten kilometre walk called "Run for the Hills." This was my first experience doing something like this. My daughter was doing the marathon run and invited me to participate with her by doing the walk. I accepted the invitation. I arrived at the race after finishing my breakfast consisting of a piece of toast and an egg. I drank my water with the hope that I would meet bathrooms along the way. Truly this was an adventure.

Runners from everywhere surrounded me. As I reached the first water station a lady called out my name and said, "Is that you Laura?" She knew me. Even though I was only a number in this race this lady knew my name.

Up the hills and against a strong wind I went and told myself that I could not slow down in the wind or I would never get my momentum up again. It seemed daunting as I looked at the long, long road ahead of me but in order to finish well I had to keep going. I saw kind people standing at various points handing out water cups with words of encouragement. They cheered, they clapped, and they played music for the purpose of getting us through the race. I was very emotional as I watched strangers cheering me on.

As I kept going on this long road I started to notice the beauty of the hills and the harvested fields. I heard the cows lowing in the far corner of a field and I saw the wonder of a wide open space of sky and land.

I absorbed the smell of bacon frying from the homes along the way as they were starting their day around their kitchen tables. I felt warm inside my heart to be a part of all of this.

The time went on and soon it was the last kilometre with the end of the race in sight. As I neared the final bend there were people announcing my name and embracing the fact that I had finished the race. I had made it home. Most of those embracing people I did not even know.

Then it dawned on me that this is the Christian life. It too is a race to run and keep running to completion. This eternal race includes a company of encouragers along the way cheering for us not to give up. We can bask in the truth that God knows our name even when the world may only call us a number. Do we notice the beautiful fragrance of people living life to the full with love and laughter? Do we notice the wonderful sight of a harvested field with its finished work as people do their assigned tasks with the abilities God has given them?

One day we will complete the race and run through the gate called home enjoying the wonder of a wide open sky and land. It will be worth it all! So run your assigned race, walk your talk, applaud another runner, and hand out the water of encouragement to all you meet. Cheer people as they get over the hills of loss, addictions, or vices and call out their names as you go. This is your race and this is the race where everyone wins!

LINGERING in the LINES – Revelation 22

A Gentleman

The title "gentleman" describes that a man should be gentle. Gentle in heart will always speak of the character of Christ. In Matthew 11:28-30 Jesus says these words, *"Come to Me, all you who are weary and burdened and I will give you rest. Take My yoke upon you and learn from Me, for I am gentle and humble in heart."*

In order to be a "gentleman" you will need to *come* to Jesus. When you *come* to Jesus you are telling God that you are willing to learn. When you are willing to learn from God you will develop a character after God's own heart. One of the character qualities of Christ is gentleness.

The only people who really learn from God are the humble people who are willing to *come*. So if you are coming to God you have already taken a leaping jump into the Kingdom of God that is within you (Luke 17:21).

Do a character test on your heart and see if you are gentle. Do you speak calmly to people even though they are frustrating you? Are you patient in answering the questions people are directing to you or are you annoyed by their questions? Do you make it a habit to say positive and encouraging words to the people around you? Take a moment to reflect on these questions and answer them. The answers you give will show you if you are becoming a "gentleman." Don't forget that you can always learn when you go to the Master of gentleness. Jesus is His name.

LINGERING in the LINES – Read about Christ in the Bible and be like Him

The Christmas Storm

The following true story was narrated to me by my mother when she was 84 years old. When she told me this story I entered it into a writing contest and she won 2nd place.

~ The stone boat was our transportation to the annual church Christmas concert. I settled the children on the floor of the sleigh. Many blankets kept them warm on this cold winter's night. My husband hitched the horses and we took the shortcut across the farmer's field. This was a path the horses knew well.

The evening ended with the sudden onset of a fierce storm. We were six miles from home. We must get home was our only thought. We again settled the children down with their blankets and set off for the shortcut across field. We were going east but lost our sense of where we were on the field that would lead us to the main road. Finally, my husband said that we would have to let the horses go on their own to find the way home. He said to me, "They know the way home."

Suddenly the horses stopped short. They knew there was a barbed wire fence in front of them and they would go no further. We redirected the horses away from the fence and they kept going. In this blizzard we could not see and continued to let the horses go on their own to lead us. The horses went on their instinct and did indeed lead us home. God leads us in so many ways. Thousands of years ago the wise men were led by a star in the east to the newborn Christ. More than 60 years ago we were led safely home by horses in a blizzard. God works in mysterious ways his wonders to perform.

~ Hannah Neufeld

A Warmed Soul

I asked my eldest son to write the first article for the New Year. As you read it, may you sense a deep and abiding peace as only the God who made all things can give you. May you this year ask God to put a spark in your soul to live life to the fullest regardless of circumstances for this always was God's chosen design for you. Now to the words of my son:

I love the start of a new year. It is a time to reflect on the past, the joy of present, and the hope for the future. However, reflecting on the past can bring hurt and remorse. The present can seem stressful and overwhelming and the future, a scary hopelessness. How come some people view their lives excitedly, while others can barely drag themselves out of bed? The key I believe is an understanding of why we exist.

As a Christian, I believe all of us were made with unique gifts and a designed purpose. Our lives and this New Year, full of opportunities is not a mistake. You are as important to God as any other human throughout the history of time. He wants to know you and be known by you. That is why you exist.

When you can come to understand that God is not wagging his big index finger at all your mistakes, but instead is embracing you and forgiving you, loving you in spite of it all, then something miraculous happens. The pressure lets go, the stress subsides and you can rest in knowledge that you are at peace with your Creator.

~ Dave Falk

A Reflective Life Story

~ Laura Falk

A wise man once said, "There is a time for everything, and a season for every activity. There is a time to weep and a time to laugh." The doctors stood beside my parents and told them to prepare for my death. I heard the conversation as I drifted in and out of consciousness and I cried out to my mother, "Am I going to die? I don't want to die." My mother was silent and did not answer my question. The vigil was beginning and they waited.

I grew up in a home of love as my heritage. As a young girl I recall many evenings when my parents would sit at the kitchen table with their Bibles. As they opened up the pages I saw my parents fall in love with the God of those pages. They were experiencing the reality of God as their own personal reality. I could see the love they had for God. It was this view that would shape my life in the days ahead as my life was soon to change forever.

I was a curious eight year old child full of little girl dreams. Without my parents knowledge I had just finished lighting a rubbish fire on the farm yard. I tried a few times to light the fire and then leaned in close to check on the progress. As I did I soon realized that the rubbish pile was burning but so was I. My little dress caught on fire and I ran screaming from pain and terror. The running fanned the flames and I was ablaze.

My brother ran towards me and put out my flaming hair with his hands saving my face from being permanently scarred. The fire was out now and I saw the outline of my slip burned into my chest. My world had suddenly changed and it would never go back to what it was. My family lovingly laid me in a clean bed sheet and transported me to the nearest country hospital. From there I was transferred to another hospital and then yet another until I was in a place that could handle the care of my extensive and life threatening burns.

The doctor told my parents I would not live to see the morning light. My father called his employer to tell him that I was not to live through the night and he would not be at work due to sitting vigil by my bedside. His employer informed him that if he did not show up for work in the morning he would be fired. We needed the income and my father had a choice to make. Love made the choice and my father chose me. That was the closest I have ever come to seeing the love of God. My father lost it all for me.

What does a parent do at a time like this when even their devoted love cannot spare the pain or determine the outcome of this life changing event? As my life changed so did theirs.

What does a mother think when she sees her perfect little girl burned beyond recognition? What does a mother do when she sees scars that will forever change the appearance of her girl? Somehow in it all she raises her heart to heaven and prays with a sacrifice of praise to the only God who can comfort the sorrowing, heal the broken, and rebuild from the ruins. This was her God and she would worship.

I was in agony. I was devastated. I was so lonely deep within my soul. I was broken. I looked out of the third story window of my hospital room and wondered what it would be like to jump from that window and end this misery.

When my father was 88 years old (he lived to be 94), he told me a story that I did not know. As I was lying on the stretcher in the ambulance my father was sitting beside me. He said that I was drifting in and out of consciousness and suddenly I awoke holding up my charred hands and said, "Oh Daddy what will I do now, I can't fold my hands to pray." My father said, "Laura, prayer is all in the heart, just pray from your heart."

As I lay suffering on my hospital bed I cried out to God from my little heart and the cry was simply, "Jesus, help me." And He did. God heard the cry and came to me. He came to me in a soft, gentle and holy whisper and called me by name and said, "Laura, I love you."

At that point I started to sing a song in my heart that my Sunday School teacher had taught me, "*Jesus loves me this I know, for the Bible tells me so. Little ones to Him belong, they are weak but He is strong. Yes, Jesus loves me, yes, Jesus loves me the Bible tells me so.*" This was now the song that I would sing and this would be the story I would tell.

I was different now. The school years were hard when I heard these words on the school bus, "Don't sit with her, she's ugly." I sat alone and yet never felt alone. God was with me. God loved me. God knew my name. I felt like God was somehow shielding me from the utter destruction of the soul. The Bible says that God is a Shield around us and I now knew that to be true in my life. My home was a safe refuge. Every time I walked into the doors of my home I felt and was completely and thoroughly loved. My parents were a balm of cheerleading support for me.

As the years progressed I soon became a wife and a mother and realized afresh and anew that dealing with our attitudes and issues is our life's work. There were many times I struggled with bad attitudes. I recall a particular time when I was reading Psalm 73 that the Word of God became flesh to me as God was showing me some attitudes that I needed to change. The Psalmist in Psalm 73 was telling God that he was like a brute beast with his embittered spirit which was senseless and ignorant before God. I felt like that too and prayed a simple prayer to God, "Lord, please change me."

I prayed for God to change me from a person who breaks easily because of insecurity and low self-worth. I asked God to change me from being a "poor me" person with a victim mentality. I begged God to change me from being a sharp edged woman who is arrogant, judgmental, and self centered. It was a simple prayer then and it still is today, "Lord, please change me." It was at that time that I made a decision to believe everything that God said in His Word. I knew that it would be God and God alone that would be the help that I would need in every attitude and issue of life.

There were several verses in Psalm 73 that were impressed on my soul then and have stayed with me all of these years even as I write this story today. The verses told me that regardless of how we struggle with wrong attitudes God will be with us always holding our hand and leading us to a better place. A life verse for me was the declaration that it was good to be near God and to make the Sovereign Lord my Refuge.

I always dreaded the day and even the thought of losing my parents. I prayed about this often and one day it happened. My father died and I was in grief, aching with the great loss of my cheerleader. After the funeral I was spending time with God and had His Word opened on my lap. I was reading in Jeremiah according to my Bible reading plan and a verse jumped off the page and into my soul. It was in Jeremiah 31:13 and reads like this, *"Then maidens will dance and be glad, young men and old as well. I will turn their mourning into gladness; I will given them comfort and joy instead of sorrow"* declares the Lord.

At that moment God released me from the sorrow and comforted me with gladness of soul. I was so thankful that I had been able to enjoy my father for many years. I was so thankful for God and His Word and its power to help us. I was thankful. I was overjoyed with God's kindness and careful watch over my soul. God turned my mourning into gladness. The next Sunday I went to church and a friend came up to me to tell me that the days ahead of grief would be harder than the days I had already walked through. I looked at her and told her that God had turned my mourning into gladness and there was nothing I could do about it.

Then four months later my mother died and I was thrust into a deeper grief than before. I dropped to the floor in my kitchen and wept with uncontrollable sobs. The grief just had to get out. I talked to God and told Him that He had turned my mourning into gladness before and asked Him if He would do it again. And He did.

I thank God for every open wound and for every healed scar because my story has given me a platform to tell the world how beautiful God is. Everyone has a wound of one kind or another.

And everyone can know and experience the God who heals those wounds with His abiding love. I received a call to speak to a group of women in a rural area close to my home. As I was preparing for this event knowing I needed to wear a skirt I told my daughter about my dislike for tight pantyhose. She quickly responded with an idea to help me. She told me about something called thigh high nylons. She told me I would never need to worry about tight pantyhose again. Her excitement for these nylons was contagious and I ran out to the local store just before the midnight close to buy these thigh high nylons.

It was the evening debut of the nylons and I got dressed in a black skirt and dressy shoes and felt good.

I was in the middle of telling my story to these women when I began to feel the slippage of my thigh high nylons down my legs. I was telling my story but my thoughts were running wild. My nylons were falling down and I was desperate. What was I to do? Just as I was about to tell the women "God loves you" out of my mouth came, "God, my nylons are falling down." It was really a prayer but the audience heard it as a declaration.

I put the microphone down to "heave ho" those nylons back up to their original thigh position. I explained that due to my daughter's great enthusiasm over these nylons I would probably have to repeat the heave ho action a few times as the evening progressed and that is exactly what I had to do.

Life takes many twists and turns with many tears and with many laughs. As a wise man once said, "There is a season for everything." There is a season to listen to the adult children and then there is a season not to at least when it comes to thigh high nylons!

I trust that as you have read my story you will see your God in a fresh new way. He really does restore the soul of a broken heart and He really does rebuild a life. He really does!

~

~A Note from Laura's Desk~

Thank you to each one of you for reading this small book. I would like to leave you with a final thought on the call of God to each one of us. That call is to pray. Jesus told us to pray. That instruction comes from God who knows all things. If God says we should pray then we should. Prayer to the God of heaven who created you is the hope for all of your issues. Prayer is the help needed for people all around the world. As a wholehearted follower of God you are on a mission. You are on a mission to pray ceaselessly, earnestly, and fervently. There is no evil power that can stop God from hearing your voice as you lift it up to the One who is attentive to your cry. You are not alone. God by His Spirit is praying with you. In prayer you are in the presence of God who tells you, "I have loved you with an everlasting love." This love is complete and it is enough to carry you through anything.

You have God as your Protector, Deliverer, Strength, Sustainer, Stronghold, Rock, Defender, Strong Support, Shield, Salvation, Everlasting Father, Fortress, and Helper.

You have God with you as your Merciful One, your Faithful One, your Living Water, your Daily Bread, your Beginning, and your End. You have God with you who is Beautiful, Majestic, All-Powerful, All-Knowing, Unchanging, Humble, Kind, and Good. You have the Most High God with you. You are safe in prayer. So pray! Pray so that you do not fall into the temptations of doubting God's truth and listening to the lies of self pursuit, the culture around you, and the evil one who desires to kill, steal, and destroy.

About Us

We have been in the bookstore business for 19 years and in all that time, change is the word that describes business to me. We always need to be fresh in how we do things in order to keep the pleasure, purpose and passion of business ownership. We expanded our business through the purchase of a building to include a café. With this expansion has come more responsibility. As in life, business is a continual learning experience.

My advice would be to always allow yourself to be taught from all life situations because they are your teachers. This learning from the teachers of life allow you to attain the wisdom that comes from God and thereby be able to accomplish more in your lives for the greater good of others. Our greatest delight in business and ministry is to have customers enjoy their shopping and eating experience.

We hope that in our business people will find a place to regroup, refresh, and restore themselves in their very busy and often chaotic lives. Our prayer is that the books we sell will bring to people "aha!" moments of clarity and true perspective on God and life.

Printed in Canada